The $27 Millionaire

HOW MARIO KELLY TURNED $27 INTO MILLIONS BY REVITALIZING COMMUNITIES AND CLEANING UP THE BUSINESS WORLD

By MARIO KELLY

All rights reserved under the international and Pan-American copyright conventions.

First published in the United States of America.

All rights reserved. With the exception of brief quotations in a review, no part of this book may be reproduced or transmitted, in any form, or by any means, electronic or mechanical (including photocopying), nor may it be stored in any information storage and retrieval system without written permission from the publisher.

DISCLAIMER

The advice contained in this material might not be suitable for everyone. The author designed the information to present his opinion about the subject matter. The reader must carefully investigate all aspects of any business decision before committing to him or herself. The author obtained the information contained herein from sources he believes to be reliable and from his own personal experience, but he neither implies nor intends any guarantee of accuracy. The author is not in the business of giving legal, accounting, or any other type of professional advice. Should the reader need such advice, he or she must seek services from a competent professional. The author particularly disclaims any liability, loss, or risk taken by individuals who directly or indirectly act on the information contained herein. The author believes the advice presented here is sound, but readers cannot hold him responsible for either the actions they take, or the risk taken by individuals who directly or indirectly act on the information contained herein.

Published by 1BrickPublishing
Printed in the United States
Copyright © 2024 by Mario Kelly
ISBN 978-1949303605

DEDICATION

This book is dedicated to the dreamers, the doers, and the believers—those who see possibility where others see obstacles, who have the courage to take that first step even when the path ahead is uncertain. To the people of Detroit, whose resilience and spirit have been a constant source of inspiration. To my family, friends, and mentors who believed in me when I didn't believe in myself. And most importantly, to every person who has ever felt overlooked or underestimated—may this story remind you that your potential is limitless, your voice matters, and your dreams are valid. This is for you. Believe in yourself, for in that belief lies the power to transform not just your own life, but the world around you.

DEDICATION REQUEST

Please share this book with anyone who you believe could benefit from its message of hope, resilience, and entrepreneurial spirit. Pass it on to those seeking to unlock their potential, make a difference in their communities, or find purpose in their work.

TABLE OF CONTENTS

Introduction: From Detroit to the Business World 1

Chapter 1: Humble Beginnings 9

Chapter 2: Hitting Rock Bottom 25

Chapter 3: The $27 Cleaning Job 41

Chapter 4: Building the Staffing Business 57

Chapter 5: Securing Big Contracts 71

Chapter 6: Cleaning Up the City 93

Chapter 7: Keys to the City 109

Chapter 8: The Future is Bright 127

Conclusion 143

Acknowledgement 159

INTRODUCTION

From Detroit to the Business World

From the streets of Detroit to the pages of this book, my journey has been one of perseverance, self-discovery, and unwavering faith in the power of the human spirit. As a young man growing up in the Motor City, I faced countless obstacles and setbacks that could have easily derailed my dreams. But through the grace of God and the support of my community, I found the strength to turn my struggles into steppingstones towards success.

My name is Mario Kelly, and I am the founder and CEO of Believe Cleaning, a company that has not only revolutionized the commercial cleaning industry but has also become a beacon of hope for countless individuals seeking a second chance at life. But my story is not just about building a successful business; it's about discovering my purpose and using my Genius-level Talent to make a difference in the world.

Growing up in Detroit, I witnessed firsthand the devastating effects of poverty, crime, and lack of opportunity on my community. I saw talented, hardworking people being forced to the margins of society, their potential left untapped and their dreams unfulfilled. It was a reality that I refused to accept, and I knew that I had to do something to change it.

As I navigated the challenges of my own life, from homelessness to divorce to financial hardship, I began to realize that my struggles were not unique. They were the struggles of countless others who had been dealt a difficult hand in life but refused to give up. It was through these experiences that I discovered my own Genius-level Talent – the ability to see potential where others saw only problems, and the drive to turn that potential into tangible results.

This book is not just my story; it's a guide for anyone who has ever felt like the odds were stacked against them. It's a testament to the power of perseverance, the importance of self-discovery, and the transformative impact of purpose-driven entrepreneurship. Through the pages of this book, I will share the lessons I have learned along the way, the principles that have guided me, and the tools that have helped me turn my vision into a reality.

At the core of my philosophy are a set of guiding principles that I call "ISMs." These ISMs are not my own creation, but rather a set of powerful philosophies I've adopted and adapted from Rocket Companies®, founded by the visionary entrepreneur Dan Gilbert. The culture found at Rocket Companies® is based on these philosophies, which they call ISMs. Pronounced iz-emz, these sayings are the core principles that drive all their decision-making and unite them around a culture of excellence.

I've been deeply inspired by these ISMs and have incorporated them into my own business and life philosophy. From "The Inches We Need Are Everywhere Around Us" to "Do The Right Thing," these ISMs have helped me navigate the complexities of entrepreneurship and stay true to my values in the face of adversity. I'm grateful to Dan Gilbert and Rocket Companies® for sharing these powerful principles, which have now become a cornerstone of my own success story.

But the ISMs are just one piece of the puzzle. To truly unlock your potential and find your purpose, you must also discover and nurture your Genius-level Talent. This is the unique combination of passion, skills, and abilities that sets you apart from everyone else and allows you to make a meaningful impact on the world. Whether you are "Word Smart," "Body Smart," or "Life Smart," your Genius-level Talent is the key to unlocking your full potential and achieving your dreams.

Throughout this book, I will guide you through the process of discovering your own Genius-level Talent and show you how to apply it in your personal and professional life. You will learn how to identify the environments, experiences, and relationships that have shaped your talents, and how to leverage those talents to create value for yourself and others.

But this book is not just about learning; it's about taking action. That's why each chapter includes practical exercises and actionable items that will help you apply the lessons learned to your own life and business. From reflecting on your personal background and experiences to brainstorming creative solutions to problems in your community, these exercises will challenge you to think differently, step outside your comfort zone, and take concrete steps towards achieving your goals.

As you embark on this journey of self-discovery and entrepreneurship, I encourage you to embrace the power of purpose. Purpose is not just about making money or achieving success; it's about using your talents and resources to make a positive impact on the world. It's about creating value not just for yourself, but for your community and for future generations.

This is the path that I have chosen, and it is the path that has led me to where I am today. Through Believe Cleaning, I have been able to provide opportunities for individuals who have been overlooked and undervalued by society. I have been able to help rebuild communities, revitalize neighborhoods, and restore hope in the hearts of those who had lost it. And I have been able to do it all by staying true to my values, the ISMs I've adopted, and my Genius-level Talent.

But my journey is far from over, and I know that there is still so much work to be done. That's why I am sharing my story and my insights with you – because I believe that together, we can create a world where everyone has the opportunity to discover their purpose and unleash their potential.

So as you read this book, I challenge you to reflect on your own journey and the experiences that have shaped you. What are the moments that have defined your life and your entrepreneurial spirit? What are the challenges that you have overcome, and what are the lessons that you have learned along the way?

Perhaps you are like me, someone who has faced adversity and hardship but refused to let it define you. Perhaps you have a vision for a better world and a burning desire to make a difference. Or perhaps you are simply searching for your place in the world and the purpose that will guide you forward.

Whatever your story may be, know that you are not alone. Know that there is a community of like-minded individuals who are ready to support you, encourage you, and help you achieve your dreams. And know that by discovering your Genius-level Talent and staying true to the ISMs, you have the power to create a life and a business that is truly extraordinary.

So let us begin this journey together. Let us explore the depths of our potential, the heights of our dreams, and the power of our purpose. Let us embrace the ISMs that will guide us forward and the Genius-level Talent that will set us apart. And let us work together to create a world where everyone has the opportunity to thrive, to succeed, and to make a difference.

Exercise: Reflect on your personal background and experiences that have shaped your entrepreneurial journey.

Take a moment to think about the moments, people, and experiences that have had the greatest impact on your life and your entrepreneurial spirit. Consider the following questions:

1. What are the challenges or obstacles that you have faced in your life, and how have they shaped your perspective and your approach to problem-solving?

2. Who are the people who have inspired you, supported you, or mentored you along the way, and what lessons have you learned from them?

3. What are the moments of triumph or achievement that have given you the confidence and the motivation to pursue your dreams?

4. What are the values, beliefs, or principles that have guided you in your personal and professional life, and how have they influenced your decisions and your actions?

5. What are the skills, talents, or abilities that you have discovered or developed over time, and how have they contributed to your success or your sense of purpose?

Take some time to reflect on these questions and write down your thoughts and insights. As you do so, look for patterns or themes that emerge, and consider how these experiences have shaped your unique perspective and your approach to entrepreneurship.

Remember, your personal background and experiences are not just a part of your past; they are the foundation upon which you can build a brighter future. By understanding and embracing your own story, you can tap into the power of your Genius-level Talent and create a life and a business that is truly authentic, meaningful, and impactful.

NOTES FROM INTRODUCTION:

CHAPTER 1

Humble Beginnings

"The Inches We Need Are Everywhere Around Us"

The cold Detroit winter air bit at my skin as I huddled in my van, surrounded by everything I owned in the world. It was early 2017, and I had hit rock bottom. Divorced, homeless, and broke, I had been evicted from my small apartment after falling behind on bills. As I pulled my coat tighter around me, trying to ward off the chill, I couldn't help but reflect on the journey that had brought me to this point.

Growing up in Detroit, I was no stranger to hardship. My childhood was a tapestry of challenges and struggles, woven together with threads of hope and resilience. My mother, a single parent, worked tirelessly to provide for my siblings and me, often juggling multiple jobs just to keep food on the table and a roof over our heads. Despite her best efforts, there were times when even these basic necessities seemed like luxuries.

Our neighborhood was a microcosm of the larger issues plaguing Detroit – high unemployment, crumbling infrastructure, and a pervasive sense of hopelessness that seemed to hang in the air like a heavy fog. But amidst this challenging environment, I found my first glimpses of opportunity and the seeds of what would later become my Genius-level Talent.

I remember the day I met Mr. Love, an entrepreneur who lived a few blocks away. He was always impeccably dressed, drove a nice car, and seemed to exude an aura of success that was rare in our part of town. One day, as I was walking home from school, I saw Mr. Love picking up litter in front of his house. Curiosity got the better of me, and I asked him why he was doing it himself instead of hiring someone.

His response changed the trajectory of my life. "Young man," he said, his eyes twinkling, "there's opportunity in everything, even in trash. You just have to be willing to see it and seize it." He then offered me a dollar for every bag of litter I could collect from around the housing project. It wasn't much, but to a kid with empty pockets and big dreams, it felt like a fortune.

That simple interaction taught me two invaluable lessons that would shape my future entrepreneurial journey. First, opportunities are everywhere, even in the most unlikely places. Second, responding with a sense of urgency can be the difference between seizing an opportunity and watching it pass you by.

I threw myself into this new "job" with enthusiasm, racing against time to fill as many bags as I could. I began to see our neighborhood in a new light. What others saw as a hopeless mess, I saw as an opportunity to make a difference – both for my community and for my own pocket. This was my first taste of the ISM "The Inches We Need Are Everywhere Around Us," though I wouldn't know it by that name until much later.

As I grew older, this ability to spot opportunities in overlooked places became more refined. I started to notice patterns – which buildings always needed cleaning, which neighbors needed help with odd jobs, which local businesses were struggling to keep up with demand. Each observation was like a piece of a puzzle, slowly revealing a bigger picture of need and opportunity in our community.

Life has a way of throwing curveballs, and my journey was far from smooth. After years of struggling to make ends meet, I had finally found some stability working at a local steel factory. The work was grueling, the hours long, and the pay modest, but it was enough to keep me afloat. I had my own small apartment and was slowly building a life for myself. It was during this time, in my early thirties, that I met Maria.

Maria was a breath of fresh air in my life. We connected instantly, sharing dreams and aspirations. For five years, we built a relationship, supporting each other through life's ups and downs. When we finally decided to get married in our mid-thirties, it felt like the culmination of years of hard work and patience.

However, the realities of life in Detroit can wear on even the strongest bonds. Just six and a half months into our marriage, everything changed. Maria unexpectedly received a $250,000 life insurance payout. This sudden windfall seemed to shift her perspective on life dramatically.

Before I could fully grasp what was happening, Maria had decided to divorce me. She wanted to live on her own, to explore a life that her newfound wealth could provide. In the blink of an eye, the dreams we had built together crumbled. When the dust settled, of the $250,000, she left me with only $1,500.

The aftermath of our divorce left me reeling. Unable to afford the apartment on my own, I soon found myself evicted, with nothing but my old van and a handful of possessions to my name. It was in this moment of absolute rock bottom that I was forced to confront the harsh realities of my life and the choices that had led me here. The woman I thought I'd spend forever with had vanished, leaving behind only legal documents and a hollowness in my chest that seemed to echo with each breath. This was my rock bottom – homeless, nearly penniless, and now, alone.

But even in this darkest hour, a small voice inside me refused to be silenced. It whispered of hope, of opportunity, of the possibility for change. This voice, I now realize, was the first stirring of my

CHAPTER 1: HUMBLE BEGINNINGS

Genius-level Talent – a unique combination of street smarts, empathy, and an unshakeable belief in the potential for transformation.

As I sat in my van that cold winter night, I made a decision. I would not be a victim of my circumstances. I would not allow my past to dictate my future. Instead, I would embrace the mindset of "Responding With A Sense Of Urgency Is The Ante To Play." I knew that if I wanted to change my life, I needed to act now, with urgency and purpose.

The next morning, I woke up with a new determination. I remembered Mr. Love's words from all those years ago about finding opportunity in unlikely places. I looked around at the bustling Eastern Market, where my mother used to sell fruit when I was young. Could this be my opportunity?

With $150 borrowed from friends and relatives, I purchased colorful rubber wristbands for seven cents apiece. I printed the phrase "BELIEVE in Detroit" on them, a message of hope not just for others, but for myself as well. I began selling these bands around town for a dollar or two, promising they'd uplift people's spirits.

To my surprise, the wristbands started to gain traction. Local rappers and minor celebrities began wearing them in Instagram posts, believing in my underdog vision. It wasn't much, but it was a start. More importantly, it was proof that opportunities really were everywhere, if only we had the eyes to see them and the courage to seize them.

As the business grew, I found myself with $17,000 in profits - a sum that felt enormous after my recent struggles. But then, an unexpected opportunity presented itself. I learned about a home that was repeatedly being fined by the city for being abandoned and unkempt. The owner, someone I knew, was struggling with the mounting fines. Seeing potential where others saw problems, I made an offer: $6,500 for the house.

It was a deal too good to pass up. I decided to invest all of my $17,000 - $6,500 for the purchase, and the rest for renovations. I planned to fix it up one room at a time, seeing it as a long-term investment in my future.

However, this decision left me broke once again. The security I thought I had built with my wristband business was gone, invested in a fixer-upper that would take time to pay off. In that moment, I had a choice. I could regret my decision, worry about the challenges ahead, and wonder if I had made a mistake. Or I could see this as yet another opportunity – a chance to build something lasting, to create a home, and to prove to myself that I could turn any situation into a success.

I chose to see the opportunity. This setback meant I had to go back on the grind to make ends meet, but it also meant I was now a homeowner, with a project that could secure my future. It was a reminder that in every challenge lies a seed of opportunity, if only we have the courage to nurture it.

CHAPTER 1: HUMBLE BEGINNINGS

As I worked to rebuild my fledgling business, I began to notice a shift in my thinking. I was no longer just looking for opportunities for myself, but for ways to create opportunities for others as well. I saw the talent and potential in my community that was going to waste, and I knew I had to do something about it.

This realization was the true awakening of my Genius-level Talent. It wasn't just about making money or achieving personal success. It was about using my unique combination of skills, experiences, and perspective to make a real difference in my community.

I started to see connections where others saw only problems. Where others saw abandoned buildings, I saw potential cleaning contracts. Where others saw unemployed youth, I saw a workforce eager for opportunity. Where others saw a city in decline, I saw a community ripe for revitalization.

This ability to see potential where others saw only problems became the cornerstone of my business philosophy. It was the driving force behind every decision I made, every risk I took, and every opportunity I pursued.

As I continued to develop this talent, I began to understand that it wasn't just about me. It was a gift, given to me by a higher power, shaped by my environment and experiences, and honed through years of struggle and perseverance. I felt a deep sense of responsibility to use this gift not just for my own benefit, but for the benefit of my community and beyond.

This realization brought with it a new sense of purpose and urgency. I knew that every day I waited was another day that someone in my community missed out on an opportunity to better their life. Every moment of hesitation was a moment wasted in the fight to revitalize Detroit.

So I threw myself into my work with renewed vigor. I started reaching out to local businesses, offering cleaning services at competitive rates. I began hiring people from my community, giving them not just jobs, but opportunities to learn, grow, and build better lives for themselves and their families.

It wasn't easy. There were countless setbacks, rejections, and moments of doubt. But with each challenge, I reminded myself of the ISM "Responding With A Sense Of Urgency Is The Ante To Play." I knew that success wasn't just about having good ideas or spotting opportunities – it was about acting on them quickly and decisively.

This mindset served me well when I attended a Detroit Youth Choir performance on NBC's America's Got Talent. As I watched these talented young people from my community shine on a national stage, an idea struck me. Why not start a t-shirt business to support their success?

I didn't have any design experience or equipment, but I knew I had to act fast if I wanted to capitalize on this opportunity. Within days, I had designed and produced a line of "BELIEVE in DYC" t-shirts. When the choir returned as hometown heroes, my shirts were there to greet them, even making an appearance during a parade broadcast on major TV networks.

This success opened up new doors and opportunities. It led to a connection with Shinola Watches, which in turn led to my first major cleaning contract. Each opportunity built on the last, creating a momentum that carried me forward.

As I reflect on this journey, I'm struck by how much of it came down to mindset. It wasn't about having more resources or better opportunities than anyone else. It was about seeing the opportunities that were already there, hidden in plain sight. It was about responding to these opportunities with urgency and determination. And it was about believing – in myself, in my community, and in the possibility of a better future.

This journey has taught me that our Genius-level Talent is not something we're born with fully formed. It's something that's shaped by our experiences, our environment, and our choices. It's a combination of the skills we develop, the perspective we gain, and the passion that drives us forward.

For me, my Genius-level Talent emerged from the crucible of my experiences. It was forged in the challenges of growing up in Detroit, tempered by the setbacks and failures I encountered along the way, and refined by my unwavering commitment to making a difference in my community.

This talent isn't just about business acumen or entrepreneurial skills. It's about seeing the world in a unique way, about connecting dots that others miss, and about having the courage to act on the opportunities we see. It's about using our gifts not just for personal gain, but for the betterment of those around us.

As I've grown my business and expanded my impact, I've come to realize that this Genius-level Talent is not static. It continues to evolve and develop as I face new challenges and opportunities. Each experience adds a new layer, a new perspective that enhances my ability to create value and make a difference.

But perhaps the most important lesson I've learned is that we all have this potential within us. We all have a unique combination of experiences, skills, and passions that give us the ability to see the world in a way that no one else can. The key is recognizing this talent, nurturing it, and having the courage to put it into action.

This is why I'm sharing my story. Not because I think I'm special or because I have all the answers, but because I believe that each of us has the potential to make a profound impact on the world around us. We just need to open our eyes to the opportunities that surround us, respond with urgency to the challenges we face, and believe in our ability to create positive change.

As you read this book and embark on your own journey of discovery and growth, I challenge you to look for the inches you need in your own life. They're everywhere around you, waiting to be noticed and seized. Whether it's a small act of kindness that brightens someone's day, a creative solution to a problem at work, or a bold idea that could transform your community – these are the inches that, when added together, can create miles of progress.

Remember, it's not about making huge leaps or dramatic changes overnight. It's about consistently taking those small steps, seizing those little opportunities, and slowly but surely building momentum towards your goals. It's about responding with urgency to the challenges and opportunities that each day brings, knowing that every action you take is an investment in your future and the future of those around you.

Your Genius-level Talent is waiting to be discovered and unleashed. It's shaped by your unique experiences, your environment, and yes, even your struggles. Embrace these elements of your journey, for they are the very things that give you a perspective that no one else has. They are the source of your unique ability to create value in the world.

As we close this chapter and move forward in our journey together, I want you to remember this: The inches you need are everywhere around you. Your job is to spot them, seize them, and use them to create the life and the impact you dream of. The world is waiting for your unique contribution. Don't keep it waiting.

Exercise: Identify small opportunities in your daily life that you can leverage to make a positive impact

Now that we've explored the concept of finding opportunities in everyday life and the importance of responding with urgency, it's time to put these ideas into practice. This exercise will help you start seeing the inches all around you and thinking about how you can leverage them to make a positive impact.

1. Observation:

For the next week, carry a small notebook with you wherever you go. As you go about your daily routine, make a conscious effort to observe your surroundings more closely. Look for things that could be improved, needs that aren't being met, or problems that need solving. These could be in your workplace, your neighborhood, or even in your own home. Write down everything you notice, no matter how small or insignificant it might seem.

2. Reflection:

At the end of each day, review your observations. Ask yourself the following questions about each one:

- Why did this catch my attention?
- Who is affected by this situation?
- What small action could I take to improve this situation?
- What resources or skills do I have that could be useful here?

3. Action Plan:

Choose three observations from your list that you feel most drawn to or capable of addressing. For each of these, develop a simple action plan:

- What specific steps can you take to make a positive impact?
- When will you take these steps?

- Who else might you need to involve or collaborate with?
- What potential obstacles might you face, and how can you overcome them?

4. Implementation:

Put your action plans into motion. Remember, the key is to respond with urgency. Don't wait for the perfect moment or until you have everything figured out. Take that first small step and build momentum from there.

5. Reflection and Iteration:

After taking action, reflect on the experience:

- What worked well?
- What challenges did you face?
- What impact did your actions have?
- What did you learn from this experience?
- How can you apply these lessons to future opportunities?

6. Sharing:

Share your experiences with others. This could be through social media, conversations with friends and family, or even by starting a blog. Sharing your journey can inspire others to look for opportunities in their own lives and create a ripple effect of positive change.

Remember, the goal isn't to solve all the world's problems overnight. It's about developing the habit of seeing opportunities for positive impact in your everyday life and responding to them with urgency. Over time, these small actions can add up to significant change, both in your life and in the lives of those around you.

As you go through this exercise, keep in mind the ISMs we've discussed:

"The Inches We Need Are Everywhere Around Us": Train your eye to spot these inches in your daily life. They might be small, but they're there if you look for them.

"Responding With A Sense Of Urgency Is The Ante To Play": Once you've identified an opportunity, don't delay. Act on it as soon as possible. Remember, urgency is the ante to play in the game of success and impact.

By consistently practicing this exercise, you'll start to develop your own Genius-level Talent for spotting and seizing opportunities. You'll become more attuned to the needs of your community and more confident in your ability to make a difference. Most importantly, you'll be taking concrete steps towards creating the positive impact you want to see in the world.

This exercise is just the beginning. As you continue on your journey, you'll find that these skills become second nature. You'll start to see opportunities everywhere you look, and you'll develop the confidence and capability to act on them effectively. This is how real change happens – not through grand gestures or overnight transformations, but through consistent, intentional actions taken day after day.

Remember, your unique experiences and perspective give you the ability to see opportunities that others might miss. Embrace this gift, nurture it, and use it to make a positive impact in your world. The inches you need are all around you – it's time to start collecting them and building your own path to success and significance.

NOTES FROM CHAPTER 1:

CHAPTER 2

Hitting Rock Bottom

"Always Raising Our Level Of Awareness"

The bitter Detroit winter had seeped into my bones as I sat in my van, staring at the stack of divorce papers on the passenger seat. The woman I thought I'd spend forever with had vanished, leaving behind only these legal documents and a hollowness in my chest that seemed to echo with each breath. This was my rock bottom – homeless, jobless, and now, alone. The cruel twist of fate cut even deeper as I realized that out of the $225,000 we had saved together over the years, she had left me with a mere $1,500. Our shared dreams, our joint efforts, our collective savings – all of it gone, leaving me with barely enough to survive a few weeks. The injustice of it all threatened to crush my spirit, but little did I know that this moment of despair would become the catalyst for an extraordinary journey of resilience and rebirth.

As I reflect on that moment, I realize that hitting rock bottom was both the worst and best thing that ever happened to me. It was the crucible in which my resilience was forged, the spark that ignited my determination to rise above my circumstances. But more importantly, it was the moment that taught me the invaluable lesson of "Always Raising Our Level Of Awareness."

In those dark days, I could have easily succumbed to despair. The temptation to give up, to blame others or circumstances for my situation, was overwhelming. But somewhere in the recesses of my mind, a voice whispered that there was more to life than this – that I had the power to change my story if only I could see beyond my current circumstances.

This realization didn't come easily or quickly. It was a gradual awakening, sparked by small moments of clarity amidst the chaos of my life. I remember one particularly cold night, huddled in my van, when I overheard a conversation between two passersby. They were discussing a local business that had recently closed down, lamenting the loss of jobs and services in the community.

As I listened, something shifted in my perception. Instead of seeing only my own problems, I began to see the broader challenges facing my community. I realized that my struggles were not unique – they were part of a larger tapestry of hardship that affected many in Detroit. This awareness opened my eyes to the possibility that in solving my own problems, I might also find ways to help others.

This shift in perspective was the first step in raising my level of awareness. It taught me that no matter how dire our circumstances might seem, there's always a bigger picture to consider. By lifting our gaze from our immediate problems, we can often find solutions or opportunities we might otherwise have missed.

As I began to practice this heightened awareness, I started noticing things I had previously overlooked. The abandoned buildings that I once saw as symbols of Detroit's decline now appeared as potential opportunities for renewal. The struggles of my neighbors, which I had previously been too preoccupied with my own problems to notice, now seemed like challenges that someone (why not me?) could address.

This new awareness also extended to myself. I began to recognize patterns in my own behavior and thinking that had contributed to my current situation. I saw how my fear of failure had often held me back from taking risks or pursuing opportunities. I realized that my tendency to say "no" to new experiences or ideas had limited my growth and potential.

It was this self-awareness that led me to adopt the "Yes Before No" philosophy. I made a conscious decision to start saying "yes" to opportunities, even when they seemed challenging or outside my comfort zone. This wasn't about being reckless or agreeing to everything that came my way. Rather, it was about approaching life with an open mind and a willingness to consider possibilities before dismissing them.

The first test of this new philosophy came when a friend suggested I try selling merchandise at local events. My initial instinct was to say no – I had no experience in retail, no startup capital, and frankly, the idea terrified me. But I caught myself before the "no" could escape my lips. Instead, I took a deep breath and said, "Yes, tell me more."

That simple "yes" led me down a path I could never have anticipated. It started with selling t-shirts at community events, which then evolved into my "BELIEVE in Detroit" wristband business. Each "yes" opened new doors, introduced me to new people, and taught me valuable lessons about business, community, and myself.

But saying "yes" wasn't always easy. Each new opportunity brought with it challenges and the potential for failure. There were many times when I doubted myself, when the voice of fear in my head screamed at me to retreat to the safety of the familiar. It was in these moments that I learned to recognize and trust my Genius-level Talent.

This talent wasn't something I was born with, nor was it something I acquired overnight. It was a unique combination of skills, instincts, and aptitudes that had been shaped by my experiences and honed through my struggles. It manifested in different ways – an enhanced memory for details that others might overlook, instincts that guided me towards opportunities, and an aptitude for connecting with people from all walks of life.

I remember the day I first truly recognized this talent in action. I was at a community meeting, listening to residents discuss their concerns about the neighborhood. As others spoke, I found my mind making connections, seeing patterns, and envisioning solutions.

Ideas flowed effortlessly, and I could clearly see how different elements could come together to address multiple issues at once.

In that moment, I realized that this wasn't just random thinking – it was my Genius-level Talent at work. My unique experiences, combined with my heightened awareness and willingness to say "yes" to new ideas, had given me a perspective that allowed me to see solutions where others saw only problems.

This realization was both exciting and humbling. Exciting because it opened up new possibilities for what I could achieve. Humbling because I understood that this talent wasn't just for my benefit – it was a tool I could use to make a real difference in my community.

As I began to consciously tap into this talent, I noticed that my memory seemed sharper. I could recall conversations, details, and ideas with remarkable clarity. This enhanced memory became a valuable asset in building relationships and spotting opportunities. I could remember people's names, their stories, their needs – information that proved invaluable as I built my business and worked to make a positive impact in the community.

My instincts, too, seemed to operate on a higher level. I found myself drawn to certain opportunities or ideas, often without fully understanding why at first. As I learned to trust these instincts, I discovered that they often led me towards successful ventures or meaningful connections.

One such instance was when I felt compelled to attend a local business networking event, despite feeling out of place and underprepared. My instincts told me that something important would come from this event, and I chose to trust that feeling. It was at this event that I met a mentor who would play a crucial role in the growth of my business, providing guidance and connections that proved invaluable.

My aptitude for learning and adapting also seemed enhanced. I found that I could quickly grasp new concepts, whether it was understanding the intricacies of running a cleaning business or learning about community development initiatives. This ability to rapidly acquire and apply new knowledge became a key factor in my ability to seize opportunities and overcome challenges.

However, recognizing and using this Genius-level Talent didn't mean that everything suddenly became easy. There were still plenty of obstacles, setbacks, and moments of doubt. But my heightened awareness, combined with my "Yes Before No" philosophy and trust in my unique talents, gave me the resilience to persist in the face of these challenges.

One of the biggest tests came when I landed my first major cleaning contract. The opportunity was far beyond anything I had done before, and a part of me was terrified that I was in over my head. But I said "yes" before my fears could say "no." I trusted my instincts, which told me that this was a pivotal moment, and

I relied on my aptitude for learning to quickly get up to speed on what I needed to know.

The contract wasn't without its challenges. There were moments when I felt overwhelmed, when the magnitude of what I had taken on seemed insurmountable. But in these moments, I leaned into my Genius-level Talent. I used my enhanced memory to keep track of the myriad details involved in the job. I trusted my instincts when making decisions about staffing and operations. And I leveraged my aptitude for learning to continually improve our processes and service quality.

As I navigated these challenges, I found that my level of awareness continued to rise. I became more attuned to the needs of my clients, the capabilities of my team, and the broader impact of our work on the community. This ever-increasing awareness allowed me to spot new opportunities, anticipate potential issues, and continually refine our approach.

It was during this time that I truly internalized the ISM "Always Raising Our Level Of Awareness." I realized that awareness isn't a static state – it's a continual process of growth and expansion. Each new experience, each challenge overcome, each lesson learned contributes to a higher level of awareness. And with each increase in awareness comes new opportunities to make a positive impact.

This understanding fundamentally changed how I approached both my business and my life. I began to see every interaction, every problem, every success as an opportunity to learn and grow. I actively sought out new experiences and perspectives, knowing that they would contribute to my expanding awareness.

I started attending community meetings not just to promote my business, but to truly listen and understand the needs and aspirations of my neighbors. I engaged with other business owners, not as competitors, but as potential collaborators and sources of knowledge. I even began to see my setbacks and failures differently – not as defeats, but as valuable lessons that would raise my awareness and prepare me for future challenges.

This approach paid off in ways I could never have imagined. As my awareness grew, so did my ability to create value for others. I began to see connections between seemingly unrelated issues in the community. I could spot emerging trends in the business world before they became obvious to others. And I could anticipate the needs of my clients and employees, often before they themselves were fully aware of them.

But perhaps the most profound impact of this growing awareness was on my sense of purpose. As I became more attuned to the interconnectedness of all things, I realized that my success was inextricably linked to the wellbeing of my community. This understanding deepened my commitment to using my business as a force for positive change.

I began to explore ways to create job opportunities for those who had been marginalized or overlooked by traditional employers. I looked for partnerships with other local businesses and organizations to maximize our collective impact. And I continually sought out new ways to give back to the community that had supported me through my darkest times.

As my business grew and my impact expanded, I never lost sight of the lessons I learned during those difficult days when I hit rock bottom. The importance of always raising our level of awareness, the power of saying "yes" to new opportunities, and the value of trusting in our unique talents – these became the guiding principles of my life and my business.

Looking back, I can see how each step of my journey contributed to the development of my Genius-level Talent. The struggles I faced gave me a unique perspective and a deep well of empathy. The risks I took honed my instincts and decision-making abilities. The diverse experiences I embraced expanded my knowledge and skills in ways I could never have planned.

But none of this would have mattered if I hadn't learned to recognize and trust in these talents. It was only when I began to consciously tap into my enhanced memory, trust my instincts, and leverage my aptitude for learning that I was able to fully realize my potential and make a meaningful impact.

This journey of self-discovery and growth is ongoing. Even now, I continue to seek out new ways to raise my awareness, to say "yes" to new opportunities, and to develop my talents. Because I've learned that there is always more to see, more to learn, more ways to grow and contribute.

As I share these experiences with you, my hope is that you'll be inspired to embark on your own journey of awareness and self-discovery. Remember, your Genius-level Talent is unique to you – shaped by your experiences, your challenges, your triumphs. It's waiting to be recognized, developed, and put into action.

So I challenge you to start raising your level of awareness today. Look beyond your immediate circumstances. Say "yes" to new experiences, even when they seem daunting. Trust your instincts and lean into your natural aptitudes. You may be surprised at the opportunities you discover and the impact you can make.

Your rock bottom, whatever it may be, doesn't have to be the end of your story. It can be the beginning – the moment when you decide to raise your awareness, embrace new possibilities, and step into your full potential. Because when you do, you'll find that the world opens up in ways you never imagined possible.

Exercise: Practice saying "yes" to new opportunities and experiences, even if they seem challenging at first

Now that we've explored the power of raising our awareness and embracing a "Yes Before No" philosophy, it's time to put these ideas into practice. This exercise is designed to help you step out of your comfort zone, raise your level of awareness, and potentially uncover new opportunities or talents you didn't know you had.

1. The 30-Day "Yes" Challenge:

For the next 30 days, commit to saying "yes" to opportunities or experiences that you would normally decline out of fear, doubt, or discomfort. This doesn't mean saying yes to everything indiscriminately, but rather being open to experiences that could potentially lead to growth or new opportunities.

2. Daily Reflection:

Each day, write down at least one thing you said "yes" to that you might have previously declined. Reflect on the following:

- What was the opportunity or experience?
- What was your initial reaction? What fears or doubts came up?
- How did you feel after saying "yes"?
- What did you learn from this experience?
- Did this experience lead to any unexpected opportunities or insights?

3. Awareness Expansion:

Make a conscious effort to expand your awareness each day. This could involve:

- Reading about a topic you're unfamiliar with
- Having a conversation with someone from a different background
- Exploring a new part of your city
- Trying a new skill or hobby

Write down one new thing you learned or observed each day as a result of this expanded awareness.

4. Talent Recognition:

As you engage in new experiences, pay attention to moments when you feel particularly energized, capable, or in "flow." These could be clues to your Genius-level Talent. Keep a record of these moments and look for patterns over time.

5. Challenging Comfort Zones:

Each week, choose one activity that significantly pushes you out of your comfort zone. This could be public speaking, networking at an event, trying a new sport, or anything that challenges you. Reflect on how this experience contributes to your personal growth and awareness.

6. Opportunity Mapping:

At the end of each week, create a mind map of the new connections, ideas, or opportunities that have arisen as a result of your "yes" philosophy and expanded awareness. How might these connect to your goals or potential business ideas?

7. Instinct Journaling:

Keep a journal of moments when you felt a strong instinct or intuition about something. Did you act on it? What was the outcome? Over time, this can help you learn to better recognize and trust your instincts.

8. Memory Exercises:

Practice using your memory more intentionally. At the end of each day, try to recall as many details as possible about your experiences, the people you met, conversations you had, etc. This can help enhance your natural memory capabilities.

9. Skill Acquisition:

Choose one new skill related to your goals or potential business ideas to work on during this 30-day period. Document your progress and reflect on how this new skill might contribute to your overall capabilities.

10. Gratitude and Growth:

Each night before bed, write down three things you're grateful for from the day, and one way you grew or stepped out of your comfort zone.

11. Final Reflection:

At the end of the 30 days, take time to reflect on your overall experience:

- How has your level of awareness changed?
- What new opportunities or insights have emerged?
- How has saying "yes" impacted your life and potential business ideas?

- What have you learned about your Genius-level Talent?
- How can you continue to apply these lessons going forward?

Remember, the goal of this exercise is not to say "yes" to everything indefinitely, but to break out of limiting patterns and raise your awareness of the opportunities around you. By the end of these 30 days, you should have a clearer sense of your capabilities, a broader perspective on potential opportunities, and increased confidence in your ability to tackle new challenges.

This exercise may feel uncomfortable at times, and that's okay. Growth often happens at the edge of our comfort zones. Trust the process, stay open to new experiences, and remember that each "yes" is a step towards uncovering your full potential and creating the impact you want to see in the world.

As you go through this exercise, keep in mind the lessons we've discussed:

"Always Raising Our Level Of Awareness": Each new experience is an opportunity to learn and grow. Stay curious and open to new perspectives.

"Yes Before No": Approach new opportunities with an open mind. Consider the potential benefits before automatically saying no out of fear or habit.

Remember, your Genius-level Talent is unique to you. It's shaped by your experiences and honed through challenges. By saying "yes" to new experiences and continually raising your awareness, you're giving yourself the opportunity to discover and develop this talent.

This exercise is just the beginning. The habits and mindset you develop over these 30 days can serve as a foundation for continued growth and opportunity throughout your life and career. Embrace the journey, trust your instincts, and stay open to the possibilities that await when you raise your awareness and say "yes" to life's opportunities.

NOTES FROM CHAPTER 2:

CHAPTER 3

The $27 Cleaning Job

"Every Client. Every Time. No Exceptions. No Excuses."

As I stood in front of the Shinola Watches headquarters, clutching my makeshift cleaning supplies, I couldn't help but feel a mix of excitement and trepidation. This was it – my first real cleaning job, a measly $27 gig that I had stumbled upon almost by accident. Little did I know that this small opportunity would be the catalyst for a life-changing journey that would not only transform my own life but also impact the lives of countless others in my community.

The path that led me to this moment was anything but straight. After the setbacks I had faced – the divorce, the homelessness, the failed wristband business – I was desperate for any opportunity to get back on my feet. It was during a tour of the Shinola facility with the Detroit Youth Choir that I noticed something that would change the course of my life.

As we were leaving the building, I spotted a cleaning crew using products that were clearly ineffective against viruses. With the recent news of a potential outbreak in China, my entrepreneurial instinct kicked in. Without thinking, I blurted out that my cleaning company could do a better job of disinfecting their space.

Of course, there was no cleaning company. It was just me, my desperation, and a spark of an idea. But something in my delivery must have resonated with the Shinola team, because they asked me to submit a bid for their cleaning services.

Panic set in as I realized the magnitude of what I had just committed to. I had no experience in commercial cleaning, no team, and certainly no supplies beyond what I could scrape together from the dollar store. But I remembered the ISM "Every Client. Every Time. No Exceptions. No Excuses." I knew that if I could land this contract, I had to deliver exceptional service, no matter what.

I spent the next 24 hours researching the commercial cleaning industry, watching YouTube tutorials, and cobbling together a business plan. When I submitted my bid, I was shocked to learn that it was significantly lower than their current contract. But instead of backing out, I saw this as an opportunity to prove myself.

Shinola took a chance on me, agreeing to a trial period. That first night, as I stood outside their building with my bucket and mop, I made a promise to myself and to them – I would deliver the best cleaning service they had ever seen, even if it killed me.

CHAPTER 3: THE $27 CLEANING JOB

And so began my journey into the world of commercial cleaning. Those first few weeks were grueling. I worked around the clock, often sleeping in my van between shifts. I scrubbed floors until my hands were raw, climbed ladders to dust hard-to-reach places, and meticulously sanitized every surface I could find.

But as exhausting as the work was, I found myself thriving. I realized that I possessed a unique combination of "Body Smart" and "People Smart" abilities that made me particularly well-suited for this industry.

My "Body Smart" intelligence manifested in my physical stamina and dexterity. I could work long hours without tiring, and I had a knack for efficient movement that allowed me to clean more effectively than others might. I found myself instinctively developing better techniques for various cleaning tasks, always looking for ways to improve my speed and effectiveness without sacrificing quality.

But it was my "People Smart" abilities that truly set me apart. I understood that cleaning wasn't just about making spaces look nice – it was about creating an environment where people felt comfortable, safe, and valued. I made a point of getting to know the Shinola employees, learning their schedules and preferences, and adjusting my cleaning routine to best accommodate their needs.

I remember one night when I overheard two employees discussing an important presentation they had the next day. Without being asked, I spent extra time that night making sure their meeting room was spotless, even going so far as to leave encouraging notes on the whiteboard. The next day, I received a heartfelt thank you from the team, who said that walking into that perfectly prepared room had given them the confidence boost they needed.

This combination of physical capability and interpersonal skills became the foundation of my approach to cleaning. I wasn't just cleaning spaces; I was creating experiences. I was solving problems before they arose. I was adding value in ways that went far beyond the basic expectations of a cleaning service.

As word of my dedication and effectiveness spread, more opportunities began to come my way. Other businesses in the building started to request my services. Soon, I found myself with more work than I could handle alone.

This growth brought new challenges. How could I maintain the level of service I had promised while expanding? How could I ensure that every client received the same exceptional experience, even when I couldn't be there personally?

It was at this point that I really internalized the ISM "Obsessed With Finding A Better Way." I knew that to grow my business without compromising on quality, I needed to constantly innovate and improve.

I started by developing a comprehensive training program for my first employees. Drawing on my "People Smart" abilities, I focused not just on teaching cleaning techniques, but on instilling the values and mindset that had made my service stand out. We didn't just clean – we problem-solved, we anticipated needs, we went above and beyond.

I also leveraged my "Body Smart" intelligence to develop more efficient cleaning methods. I studied ergonomics to find ways to clean that were less physically taxing, allowing us to work longer and more effectively. I experimented with different tools and products, always seeking the most effective and environmentally friendly options.

But my obsession with improvement didn't stop there. I began to look at the bigger picture of what we were doing. I realized that our work had the potential to impact not just the cleanliness of spaces, but the overall well-being of the people who used them.

This realization led me to expand our services beyond just cleaning. We started offering workplace organization consultations, helping businesses create more efficient and enjoyable work environments. We developed custom cleaning plans for each client, taking into account their unique needs and challenges.

I also saw an opportunity to make a difference in my community. I began to actively recruit and train individuals who had struggled to find employment elsewhere – people with criminal records, those recovering from addiction, single parents struggling to make ends meet. I knew from my own experience how transformative a second chance could be, and I was determined to pay that forward.

This approach not only allowed us to grow our business, but it also created a ripple effect of positive change in our community.

Our employees, given the opportunity and support they needed, became some of our most dedicated and effective team members. Many went on to take on leadership roles within the company, or even start their own businesses.

As our reputation grew, so did the scale of our contracts. From that initial $27 job at Shinola, we expanded to cleaning entire office buildings, then stadiums, and eventually even secured contracts with major corporations and government buildings.

But no matter how big we got, I never forgot the principles that got us there. "Every Client. Every Time. No Exceptions. No Excuses" remained our mantra. Whether we were cleaning a small office or a massive stadium, we approached each job with the same level of dedication and attention to detail.

I remember one particularly challenging contract we secured with a large corporate client. They had been through several cleaning companies, none of which had met their exacting standards. On our first night, we encountered a mess that would have sent most cleaning crews running – a major spillage that had seeped into carpets and under furniture.

Instead of seeing this as a problem, we saw it as an opportunity to showcase our capabilities. I personally led the team that night, drawing on every ounce of my "Body Smart" and "People Smart" abilities. We worked through the night, not just cleaning the visible mess but deep cleaning the entire office.

When the client's employees arrived the next morning, they were stunned. Not only was the spillage completely gone, but the entire office looked and smelled better than it ever had. We had rearranged furniture for more efficient cleaning, left personalized notes for employees about how to maintain their spaces, and even fixed a few minor maintenance issues we had noticed along the way.

This experience became a turning point for our business. The client, impressed by our go-above-and-beyond attitude, not only retained our services but also recommended us to several other large corporations. It was a testament to the power of our commitment to exceptional service, no matter the circumstances.

As our business continued to grow, I never lost sight of the importance of continuous improvement. We invested heavily in training and development for our team members, encouraging them to contribute their own ideas for how we could do things better. We stayed on top of the latest cleaning technologies and techniques, always looking for ways to improve our efficiency and effectiveness.

But perhaps most importantly, we never lost our connection to the human side of our work. We remembered that behind every dirty floor or dusty desk was a person – someone who deserved to work in a clean, healthy environment. We saw our work not just as cleaning, but as creating spaces where people could thrive.

This human-centered approach extended to how we treated our own team members. We provided fair wages, comprehensive benefits, and opportunities for advancement. We created a culture of respect and empowerment, where every team member felt valued and heard.

As I reflect on the journey from that first $27 job to where we are now, I'm struck by how much of our success came down to the application of those two key intelligences – "Body Smart" and "People Smart" – combined with an unwavering commitment to service and continuous improvement.

Our "Body Smart" abilities allowed us to perform our work with a level of efficiency and effectiveness that set us apart from our competitors. But it was our "People Smart" abilities that truly made the difference. We didn't just clean spaces; we built relationships. We didn't just meet expectations; we anticipated needs. We didn't just solve problems; we prevented them from occurring in the first place.

And through it all, we remained "Obsessed With Finding A Better Way." Whether it was developing new cleaning techniques, improving our training programs, or finding innovative ways to serve our community, we never stopped pushing ourselves to improve.

This journey has taught me that success in business – and in life – is about more than just technical skills or business acumen. It's about understanding and leveraging your unique abilities, staying committed to your values, and always striving to make a positive impact.

As I look to the future, I'm excited about the possibilities that lie ahead. We're exploring new technologies that could revolutionize the cleaning industry. We're developing programs to help other entrepreneurs from disadvantaged backgrounds start their own businesses. And we're continually looking for new ways to make a positive impact in our community.

But no matter how much we grow or how much success we achieve, I'll never forget the lessons learned from that first $27 job. Every client, every time, no exceptions, no excuses. That's the foundation upon which we've built our success, and it's the principle that will continue to guide us into the future.

Exercise: Identify your "Body Smart" and "People Smart" abilities and brainstorm ways to apply them in your business or career

Now that we've explored how leveraging "Body Smart" and "People Smart" abilities can lead to success in business, it's time for you to identify and harness your own unique capabilities. This exercise will help you recognize your strengths in these areas and find innovative ways to apply them in your professional life.

Part 1: Identifying Your "Body Smart" Abilities

1. Physical Awareness:

- Take a few minutes to tune into your body. What physical activities do you excel at?
- Are you particularly coordinated, strong, flexible, or have good endurance?
- Do you have a keen sense of spatial awareness or balance?

2. Kinesthetic Learning:

    - Think about how you learn best. Do you prefer hands-on experiences?
    - Are you good at learning new physical skills or movements quickly?
    - Do you find yourself fidgeting or moving while thinking or problem-solving?

3. Non-verbal Communication:

    - How adept are you at reading body language?
    - Are you good at expressing yourself through gestures or facial expressions?
    - Can you easily mimic others' movements or mannerisms?

4. Physical Problem-solving:

    - Are you good at figuring out how things work mechanically?
    - Do you enjoy puzzles or games that involve physical manipulation?
    - Are you the person others call when something needs to be fixed or assembled?

Part 2: Identifying Your "People Smart" Abilities

1. Emotional Intelligence:

    - How well can you read others' emotions?

- Are you good at managing your own emotions in challenging situations?
- Can you easily empathize with others' experiences?

2. Communication Skills:

- Are you a good listener?
- Can you express your ideas clearly and persuasively?
- Are you adept at mediating conflicts or misunderstandings?

3. Relationship Building:

- Do you easily form connections with new people?
- Are you good at maintaining long-term relationships?
- Can you work effectively with a diverse group of people?

4. Leadership and Influence:

- Are you able to motivate and inspire others?
- Can you effectively delegate tasks and manage teams?
- Are you good at persuading others or building consensus?

Part 3: Applying Your Abilities

Now that you've identified your "Body Smart" and "People Smart" strengths, it's time to think about how you can leverage these in your business or career.

1. Current Role Analysis:

- List your current job responsibilities or business activities.

- For each responsibility, note how you could better incorporate your "Body Smart" and "People Smart" abilities.

2. New Opportunities:

- Brainstorm at least five new initiatives or projects in your field that would allow you to fully utilize your identified strengths.

3. Skill Development:

- Based on your analysis, identify areas where you could further develop your "Body Smart" and "People Smart" abilities to enhance your professional effectiveness.
- Create a plan to improve these skills over the next 3-6 months.

4. Value Proposition:

- Craft a brief "elevator pitch" that highlights how your unique combination of "Body Smart" and "People Smart" abilities adds value to your organization or clients.

5. Innovation Ideas:

- Think about the challenges in your industry. How could your specific "Body Smart" and "People Smart" abilities be used to address these challenges in innovative ways?

6. Collaboration Opportunities:

    - Identify colleagues or potential partners whose "Body Smart" and "People Smart" abilities complement your own. How could you collaborate to create something greater than the sum of its parts?

7. Customer/Client Experience:

    - Consider how you could use your "Body Smart" and "People Smart" abilities to enhance the experience of your customers or clients.
    - Develop three specific ideas to implement in the next month.

8. Personal Brand:

    - Reflect on how your unique combination of "Body Smart" and "People Smart" abilities sets you apart in your field.
    - Develop a personal brand statement that encapsulates these strengths.

9. Future Vision:

    - Imagine your ideal career or business five years from now. How would it fully utilize and showcase your "Body Smart" and "People Smart" abilities?
    - What steps can you take now to move towards this vision?

10. Action Plan:

- Based on all your reflections and ideas, create a concrete action plan for the next 90 days.
- Include specific goals, action steps, and deadlines for leveraging your "Body Smart" and "People Smart" abilities more effectively in your professional life.

Remember, the key to success is not just identifying your strengths, but actively finding ways to apply them in your work. Be creative, be bold, and don't be afraid to step out of your comfort zone. Your unique combination of "Body Smart" and "People Smart" abilities is your superpower – use it to set yourself apart and make a real impact in your field.

As you work through this exercise, keep in mind the ISMs we've discussed:

"Every Client. Every Time. No Exceptions. No Excuses": How can you apply your abilities to consistently deliver exceptional value?

"Obsessed With Finding A Better Way": How can you use your unique strengths to innovate and improve in your field?

By actively leveraging your "Body Smart" and "People Smart" abilities, you're not just improving your own career prospects – you're positioning yourself to make a meaningful difference in your industry and beyond. Embrace your unique talents, continually seek ways to apply them, and watch as new opportunities unfold before you.

NOTES FROM CHAPTER 3:

CHAPTER 4

Building the Staffing Business

"It's Not About WHO Is Right; It's About WHAT Is Right."

As our cleaning business began to thrive, I found myself faced with a new challenge – one that would test not only my business acumen but also my commitment to my community. The demand for our services was growing rapidly, and with it, the need for more staff. But as I looked around at the unemployment rates in Detroit, particularly in the neighborhoods I grew up in, I realized that this challenge was also an opportunity.

I remembered the words of Mr. Love, the entrepreneur who gave me my first job picking up litter: "There's opportunity in everything, even in trash. You just have to be willing to see it and seize it." Now, I saw an opportunity not just to grow my business, but to make a real difference in my community.

This realization led me to expand our business model to include staffing services. But this wasn't going to be just another temp agency. I wanted to create something that would truly serve the needs of our community while also meeting the demands of our clients.

The decision to move into staffing wasn't an easy one. There were voices – both internal and external – that cautioned against it. Some argued that we should stick to what we knew, that branching out into staffing was too risky. Others worried that hiring from disadvantaged communities would lead to unreliable workers and dissatisfied clients.

But as I wrestled with these concerns, I kept coming back to the ISM "It's Not About WHO Is Right; It's About WHAT Is Right." This principle challenged me to look beyond personal opinions or conventional wisdom and focus on what would truly be best for our business and our community.

I knew in my heart that creating job opportunities for those who had been overlooked or marginalized was the right thing to do. But I also believed that with the right approach, it could be good for our business too. After all, who would be more motivated and loyal than employees who had been given a second chance?

So, we took the plunge. We started small, placing individuals referred by nonprofit partners into basic facilities roles. We provided comprehensive training, transportation assistance, and even uniforms to ensure they had everything they needed to succeed.

It wasn't easy at first. Some of our new hires struggled with the transition to regular employment. Issues like punctuality, professional conduct, and consistency were challenges for those who had been out of the workforce for extended periods.

But we didn't give up. We doubled down on our training efforts, developed mentorship programs, and worked closely with each individual to address their specific needs and challenges. We recognized that for many of our new employees, this wasn't just a job – it was a lifeline, a chance to rebuild their lives and provide for their families.

As we worked through these challenges, I found myself drawing on my "Self Smart" and "Life Smart" abilities in ways I never had before. My "Self Smart" intelligence allowed me to stay true to my values and vision, even when faced with setbacks or criticism. I knew that what we were doing was right, not just for our business, but for our community as a whole.

My "Life Smart" abilities came into play as we developed programs to support our employees beyond just providing a paycheck. We created financial literacy workshops, counseling services, and career development programs. We recognized that for many of our employees, the challenges they faced extended far beyond the workplace, and we were committed to supporting them holistically.

This approach, while challenging, began to pay off. As our employees felt supported and valued, their performance improved. They became more reliable, more skilled, and more invested in their work. Our clients began to take notice, commenting on the positive attitudes and strong work ethic of our staff.

One particular success story stands out in my mind is Antonio Scales, a young man who came to us with a history of incarceration and substance abuse. Many employers wouldn't have given him a second glance. But we saw potential in Antonio – a spark of determination and a willingness to learn.

We started Antonio on basic cleaning tasks, but he quickly showed an aptitude for more complex work. We provided him with additional training, and within six months, he had become one of our most skilled and reliable employees. A year later, Antonio was promoted to team leader, responsible for managing a crew of his own.

Antonio's story wasn't unique. As word spread about our program, we began to receive more and more applications from individuals who had struggled to find employment elsewhere. Ex-offenders, recovering addicts, single parents, and others who had been marginalized by traditional hiring practices found a home with us.

But as our staffing business grew, so did the challenges. We faced skepticism from some clients who were hesitant to work with individuals with checkered pasts. We had to navigate complex regulations and compliance issues. And we had to constantly balance our social mission with the need to run a profitable business.

It was during this time that I really internalized the "We Are The 'They'" philosophy. I realized that we couldn't view our employees, our clients, or even our competitors as separate from us. We were all part of the same community, all working towards the same goal of a better, more prosperous Detroit.

This mindset shift had a profound impact on how we operated. Instead of seeing our employees as just workers, we saw them as partners in our mission. We implemented profit-sharing programs and created pathways for employees to advance within the company. We encouraged open communication and actively sought input from all levels of the organization.

With our clients, we moved beyond a transactional relationship to become true partners in their success. We were transparent about our mission and our methods, inviting clients to be part of the transformative work we were doing. Many of our clients became enthusiastic supporters, offering additional opportunities and resources to support our employees.

Even with our competitors, we sought collaboration rather than conflict. We shared best practices, partnered on large projects, and worked together to advocate for policies that would benefit our industry and our community as a whole.

This collaborative approach, combined with our commitment to doing what was right, began to yield remarkable results. Our business continued to grow, but more importantly, we were making a real difference in people's lives and in our community.

We saw former employees start their own businesses, becoming job creators themselves. We witnessed families stabilized, neighborhoods revitalized, and a renewed sense of hope in communities that had long been neglected.

But perhaps the most profound impact was the shift in perception. As our employees proved themselves time and time again, we began to challenge the stereotypes and biases that had held so many people back. Employers who had once been skeptical about hiring individuals with criminal records or gaps in their employment history were now actively seeking out our staffing services.

This success allowed us to expand our impact even further. We began partnering with local schools and community colleges to create job training programs. We worked with policymakers to advocate for fair chance hiring practices. We even started a microloan program to help our employees start their own small businesses.

Throughout this journey, I never lost sight of the principle that guided us from the beginning: "It's Not About WHO Is Right; It's About WHAT Is Right." Every decision we made, every policy we implemented, every partnership we formed was evaluated not based on who proposed it or who would get the credit, but on whether it was the right thing to do for our business, our employees, and our community.

This commitment to doing what's right hasn't always been easy. There have been times when it would have been simpler or more profitable in the short term to take a different path. But I've learned that when you stay true to your values and focus on creating value for others, success follows.

As I reflect on our journey, I'm filled with a deep sense of gratitude and purpose. What started as a small cleaning business born out of necessity has grown into a force for positive change in our community. We've created jobs, restored dignity, and kindled hope in places where it had long been extinguished.

But I also know that our work is far from over. There are still too many people in our community who are struggling, too many barriers to opportunity that need to be broken down. As we look to the future, we remain committed to our mission of creating opportunities and transforming lives.

We're exploring new ways to expand our impact, from developing technology platforms to connect job seekers with opportunities, to partnering with other businesses to create apprenticeship programs. We're also looking at how we can replicate our model in other cities facing similar challenges.

Through it all, we'll continue to be guided by the principles that have brought us this far. We'll keep focusing on what's right, not who's right. We'll continue to see ourselves as part of a larger "we," working collaboratively to create positive change. And we'll never stop looking for better ways to serve our employees, our clients, and our community.

As I share this story, my hope is that it will inspire others to look beyond conventional business models and consider how they can use their skills, resources, and influence to make a positive impact. Whether you're a business owner, a manager, or an employee, you have the power to make choices that prioritize the greater good.

Remember, true success isn't just about profits or personal gain. It's about creating value, lifting others up, and leaving the world a little better than you found it. When we approach our work with this mindset, we not only build more successful businesses – we build stronger communities and a brighter future for all.

Exercise: Reflect on your decision-making process and consider how you can prioritize the greater good in your choices

This exercise is designed to help you evaluate your current decision-making process and find ways to incorporate a greater focus on the collective good. By the end of this exercise, you should have a clearer understanding of how your choices impact others and how you can make decisions that benefit both your personal or business goals and the wider community.

1. Decision Inventory:

Take a week to keep a log of all the significant decisions you make, both in your personal life and in your work. For each decision, note:

- What the decision was about
- What factors you considered
- Who was affected by the decision
- What the outcome was

2. Impact Analysis:

Review your decision log and for each decision, consider:

- Did this decision have any impact beyond yourself or your immediate team?
- Were there any unintended consequences, positive or negative?
- Could the decision have been made differently to create a more positive impact?

3. Stakeholder Mapping:

For your work or business, create a map of all the stakeholders who are impacted by your decisions. This might include:

- Employees
- Customers
- Suppliers
- Local community
- Environment
- Future generations

4. Values Clarification:

Write down your personal values and the values of your organization (if applicable). Consider:

- How well do your day-to-day decisions align with these values?

- Are there any values that you'd like to prioritize more in your decision-making?

5. Greater Good Scenarios:

Create three hypothetical scenarios relevant to your work or business where there's a conflict between short-term gain and long-term benefit to the greater good. For each scenario:

- What would be the easy or conventional decision?
- What would be the decision that prioritizes the greater good?
- What might be the short-term and long-term consequences of each choice?

6. Decision-Making Framework:

Based on your reflections, develop a personal framework for making decisions that prioritize the greater good. This might include questions like:

- Who will be impacted by this decision?
- How does this align with my/our values?
- What are the long-term consequences?
- Is there a way to create value for multiple stakeholders?

7. Collaborative Decision-Making:

Identify three upcoming decisions in your work or business where you could involve more stakeholders in the decision-making process. Plan how you will gather input and incorporate diverse perspectives.

8. Learning from Others:

Research and write about three examples of leaders or organizations who have made tough decisions that prioritized the greater good over short-term gain. What can you learn from their approach?

9. Personal Commitment:

Based on everything you've reflected on, write a personal commitment statement about how you will prioritize the greater good in your decision-making going forward. Be specific about the changes you plan to make.

10. Action Plan:

Develop a 30-day action plan to implement your new decision-making approach. This might include:

- Sharing your commitment with your team or colleagues
- Scheduling regular time for reflection on your decisions
- Setting up systems to gather more diverse input on key decisions
- Identifying a mentor or accountability partner to support your growth in this area

11. Reflection and Iteration:

After 30 days, review your progress. Consider:

- How has your decision-making process changed?
- What impact have you observed from these changes?
- What challenges did you face, and how can you overcome them?
- How can you continue to refine and improve your approach?

Remember, shifting your decision-making process to prioritize the greater good is a journey, not a destination. It requires ongoing reflection, learning, and adjustment. But by consistently focusing on creating value for others and considering the broader impact of your choices, you can become a force for positive change in your organization and community.

As you work through this exercise, keep in mind the ISMs we've discussed:

"It's Not About WHO Is Right; It's About WHAT Is Right": Focus on the merit of ideas and their potential impact, rather than on who proposed them or who might get credit.

"We Are The 'They'": Remember that you're not separate from your community or stakeholders. Your decisions impact a web of interconnected people and systems.

By incorporating these principles into your decision-making process, you can create a ripple effect of positive change that extends far beyond your immediate sphere of influence. You'll not only build a more successful and sustainable business or career, but you'll also contribute to building a better world for all.

NOTES FROM CHAPTER 4:

CHAPTER 5

Securing Big Contracts

"You'll See It When You Believe It."

As our cleaning and staffing business continued to grow, I found myself standing at the precipice of a new challenge. We had built a solid reputation in Detroit, servicing small to medium-sized businesses and making a real difference in our community. But I knew that to truly scale our impact, we needed to secure bigger contracts – the kind that could provide stable, long-term employment for hundreds of people.

The prospect was both exhilarating and terrifying. On one hand, I was filled with excitement at the potential to create more opportunities and make an even bigger impact. On the other hand, I was gripped by a nagging sense of self-doubt. Who was I, a former homeless man with no formal business education, to think I could compete for contracts with major corporations and government entities?

This internal struggle was my first real encounter with impostor syndrome. Despite all we had achieved, a part of me still felt like a fraud – like at any moment, someone would realize I didn't belong in these high-stakes business negotiations.

It was during this time of self-doubt that I remembered the ISM "You'll See It When You Believe It." This simple yet profound statement became my mantra as I grappled with my fears and insecurities. I realized that if I couldn't believe in myself and our capabilities, how could I expect potential clients to believe in us?

I knew I had to overcome this mental barrier if we were going to move forward. So, I started practicing daily affirmations, reminding myself of all we had accomplished and the lives we had changed. I visualized myself confidently presenting our proposals to corporate executives and winning those big contracts.

Slowly but surely, my confidence began to grow. I started to see myself not as an imposter, but as a visionary entrepreneur with a unique perspective and valuable experience to offer. This shift in mindset was crucial as we began to pursue larger contracts.

Our first big opportunity came when we heard about a request for proposals from a major automotive manufacturer. They were looking for a company to handle cleaning and facilities management for their headquarters and several production plants. It was a massive contract, far bigger than anything we had tackled before.

My initial instinct was to hesitate. Were we ready for something this big? What if we bit off more than we could chew? But then I remembered another important ISM: "Take The Roast Out Of The Oven." This principle reminded me that perfection is not the goal when it's time to make a decision. Sometimes, you need to move forward with what you have, even if it's not perfect.

With this in mind, I gathered our team and we got to work on the proposal. This is where my "Word Smart" and "Reasoning Smart" abilities really came into play. I knew that to win this contract, we needed to do more than just offer competitive pricing – we needed to tell a compelling story and present a logical, well-reasoned argument for why our company was the best choice.

I drew on my "Word Smart" skills to craft a narrative that went beyond the typical business proposal. We didn't just talk about our cleaning capabilities; we shared our vision for how we could partner with the company to create a cleaner, more efficient work environment that would boost productivity and employee satisfaction. We told the stories of our employees – how our company had given them a second chance and how their dedication and work ethic would benefit the client.

My "Reasoning Smart" abilities came into play as we developed our operational plan and pricing structure. We conducted thorough research on the client's needs and the specific challenges of cleaning and maintaining automotive facilities. We created detailed projections showing how our approach would save the company money in the long run through increased efficiency and reduced employee turnover.

As we worked on the proposal, I continually reminded our team to believe in our capabilities. "You'll see it when you believe it," I told them. "We have something unique to offer, and we need to believe in that with every fiber of our being."

The day of the presentation arrived, and as I stood before the panel of executives, I felt a sense of calm confidence. I believed in what we were offering, and that belief shone through in every word I spoke and every slide I presented.

To our amazement and delight, we won the contract. It was a transformative moment for our company, opening doors to opportunities we had only dreamed of before. But more importantly, it was a powerful lesson in the importance of self-belief and the willingness to take calculated risks.

This success gave us the confidence to pursue other large contracts. We began bidding on government contracts, expanding into new industries, and even exploring opportunities in other cities. With each new contract we secured, our belief in ourselves and our mission grew stronger.

But it wasn't always smooth sailing. There were times when we faced setbacks and rejections. I remember one particularly disappointing loss – a contract we had worked on for months and felt certain we would win. When the news came that we hadn't been selected, it would have been easy to let doubt creep back in.

Instead, we chose to view it as a learning opportunity. We reached out to the client for feedback, determined to understand where we could improve. This proactive approach not only helped us refine our proposals for future bids but also impressed the client. Six months later, when another opportunity arose with their company, they specifically requested that we submit a proposal.

This experience taught us another valuable lesson – that setbacks and failures are not endpoints, but stepping stones on the path to success. Each challenge we faced made us stronger, smarter, and more resilient.

As we continued to grow and take on larger contracts, I found myself consistently drawing on my "Word Smart" and "Reasoning Smart" abilities. In negotiations, I used my language skills to articulate our value proposition clearly and persuasively. In developing new service offerings, I applied logical reasoning to identify client needs and create innovative solutions.

One of our biggest breakthroughs came when we secured a contract with a major healthcare provider. They were looking for more than just a cleaning service – they needed a partner who could help them maintain the highest standards of cleanliness and safety across their network of hospitals and clinics.

This contract required us to level up in every way. We had to become experts in healthcare-specific cleaning protocols, invest in new equipment and training, and scale our operations significantly. It was a daunting challenge, but one we embraced wholeheartedly.

I remember sitting with our team, mapping out how we would approach this contract. We were venturing into uncharted territory, and I could sense the mix of excitement and apprehension in the room. That's when I reminded everyone of our guiding principle: "You'll see it when you believe it."

"We may not have all the answers right now," I told them, "but I believe in our ability to figure it out. We've overcome every challenge we've faced so far, and we'll overcome this one too. Let's visualize success and then work backwards to determine how we'll achieve it."

This approach – combining unwavering belief with practical planning – became our blueprint for tackling every new challenge. We visualized success, believed in our ability to achieve it, and then applied our "Reasoning Smart" skills to develop a concrete plan of action.

Executing the healthcare contract was not without its difficulties. We faced a steep learning curve, encountered unexpected obstacles, and had to quickly adapt to the unique demands of the healthcare environment. But our belief in ourselves and our mission never wavered.

We poured ourselves into training, brought in experts to advise us, and worked tirelessly to exceed our client's expectations. Our employees, many of whom had never worked in such a high-stakes environment before, rose to the challenge magnificently. They took pride in knowing that their work was directly contributing to patient health and safety.

As we successfully delivered on this contract, word began to spread in the healthcare industry. Other hospitals and healthcare providers started reaching out to us, impressed by the results we had achieved. Suddenly, we found ourselves positioned as specialists in healthcare facility management – a niche we had never even considered when we started our journey.

This experience taught us the power of believing in possibilities beyond our current reality. By having the courage to step into a new industry and the confidence to believe we could excel in it, we had opened up a whole new world of opportunities.

Throughout this period of growth and expansion, I never lost sight of our core mission – to create opportunities for those who had been marginalized or overlooked. As we took on bigger contracts and entered new industries, we continually looked for ways to bring more people from our community along on this journey of growth.

We developed specialized training programs to prepare our employees for the unique demands of each new contract. We created mentorship systems where experienced team members could guide and support newer employees. And we continued to prioritize hiring individuals who had faced barriers to employment, believing in their potential just as others had believed in mine.

One story that stands out in my mind is that of Maria, a single mother who joined our company as a part-time cleaner. When we won the healthcare contract, Maria expressed interest in taking on more responsibility. Despite her lack of experience in the healthcare sector, we saw her potential and invested in her training.

Maria threw herself into learning everything she could about healthcare cleaning protocols. She worked extra hours, studied in her free time, and quickly became one of our most knowledgeable team members in this area. Within a year, she had been promoted to team leader, overseeing a crew responsible for maintaining an entire hospital wing.

Stories like Maria's reinforced my belief in the power of opportunity and the untapped potential within our communities. They also strengthened my resolve to continue pushing for bigger contracts and greater impact.

As our reputation grew and we began to be invited to bid on even larger contracts, I found myself in boardrooms and negotiations that I could never have imagined when I was living in my van just a few years earlier. There were times when the impostor syndrome threatened to resurface, when I looked around at the corporate executives in their expensive suits and felt out of place.

But in those moments, I would remind myself of all we had accomplished and the lives we had changed. I would think of Maria, and all the other employees whose lives had been transformed through the opportunities we provided. And I would silently repeat to myself, "You'll see it when you believe it."

This unwavering belief, combined with the practical application of our "Word Smart" and "Reasoning Smart" abilities, became our secret weapon in securing major contracts. We weren't just selling cleaning services – we were offering a partnership that could transform their operations and make a positive impact on their communities.

In our proposals and presentations, we used our "Word Smart" skills to paint a vivid picture of the value we could bring. We didn't just talk about cleaning schedules and staff numbers – we told stories of transformation, both of spaces and of lives. We used language that resonated with our clients' values and aspirations, positioning ourselves not just as a vendor, but as a partner in achieving their goals.

Our "Reasoning Smart" abilities came into play as we developed customized solutions for each potential client. We didn't offer one-size-fits-all packages, but rather took the time to understand each client's unique challenges and objectives. We then used logical reasoning to develop innovative approaches that would address their specific needs while also aligning with our mission and capabilities.

This combination of emotional resonance and logical problem-solving proved to be incredibly effective. Clients were drawn in by our passion and our purpose, and then convinced by the soundness of our plans and the evidence of our past successes.

As we continued to secure bigger contracts and expand our operations, I never lost sight of the importance of believing in ourselves and our mission. I made it a priority to regularly communicate our vision and our achievements to our entire team, from the newest cleaner to the most experienced manager.

We celebrated every victory, no matter how small, and used every setback as a learning opportunity. We created a culture where everyone was encouraged to believe in themselves and in our collective ability to overcome any challenge.

This belief became a self-fulfilling prophecy. The more we believed in our ability to take on bigger challenges and make a greater impact, the more we were able to achieve. Our confidence attracted more opportunities, and our track record of success gave us the credibility to pursue even larger contracts.

Looking back on our journey from a small, local cleaning company to a major player in the facilities management industry, I'm struck by how much of our success came down to the power of belief. Belief in ourselves, belief in our mission, and belief in the potential of every individual we employed.

This journey has taught me that success is not just about skills, resources, or even opportunities. It's about having the courage to believe in a vision of what's possible, even when others can't see it yet. It's about having the confidence to step into spaces where you might not feel you belong, knowing that your unique perspective and experiences have value.

As we look to the future, I'm filled with excitement about the possibilities that lie ahead. We're exploring new industries, developing innovative service models, and always looking for ways to create more opportunities for those who need them most.

But no matter how big we grow or how much success we achieve, I'll never forget the lesson that has brought us this far: "You'll see it when you believe it." This principle will continue to guide us as we face new challenges and pursue even bigger dreams.

To all the aspiring entrepreneurs and change-makers out there, I say this: Believe in yourself and your vision, even when others doubt. Take risks, even when they seem daunting. And remember, every big achievement starts with the belief that it's possible.

Your unique experiences, your passion, and your perspective are your superpowers. Believe in them, nurture them, and use them to make the impact only you can make. The world is waiting for your contribution – believe in it, and you will see it become reality.

Exercise: Practice self-affirmation and visualize yourself achieving your goals, no matter how big they may seem

This exercise is designed to help you harness the power of self-belief and visualization to overcome self-doubt and achieve your goals.

By regularly practicing these techniques, you can build your confidence, clarify your objectives, and motivate yourself to take action towards your dreams.

1. Self-Affirmation Practice:

a. Identify Your Strengths:

- Make a list of your top 10 strengths, skills, or positive qualities.
- Include both personal and professional attributes.
- Ask friends, family, or colleagues for input if you're struggling to identify your strengths.

b. Create Positive Affirmations:

- For each strength or quality, create a positive affirmation.
- Use present tense, first-person statements.
- Example: "I am a creative problem-solver" or "I am capable of overcoming any challenge."

c. Daily Affirmation Ritual:

- Choose 3-5 affirmations to focus on each day.
- Spend 5 minutes each morning and evening repeating these affirmations to yourself.
- Say them out loud, with conviction, while looking at yourself in a mirror if possible.

d. Affirmation Journal:

- Keep a journal where you write your daily affirmations.
- After each week, reflect on how these affirmations have influenced your thoughts and actions.

2. Goal Visualization Exercise:

a. Identify Your Goals:

- Write down 3-5 significant goals you want to achieve in the next 1-5 years.
- Be specific and ambitious – remember, "You'll see it when you believe it."

b. Create a Detailed Vision:

- For each goal, write a detailed description of what success looks like.
- Include sensory details – what will you see, hear, feel, etc. when you achieve this goal?
- Describe how achieving this goal will impact your life and the lives of others.

c. Visualization Practice:

- Spend 10 minutes each day visualizing yourself achieving these goals.
- Find a quiet place where you won't be disturbed.

- Close your eyes and create a vivid mental image of your success.
- Engage all your senses in this visualization.
- Allow yourself to feel the positive emotions associated with achieving your goals.

d. Vision Board:

- Create a physical or digital vision board representing your goals.
- Include images, words, and symbols that represent your aspirations.
- Place this vision board where you'll see it daily.

3. Overcoming Self-Doubt:

a. Identify Limiting Beliefs:

- Write down any negative thoughts or beliefs that are holding you back.
- Example: "I'm not qualified enough" or "I don't have the resources to succeed."

b. Challenge and Reframe:

- For each limiting belief, write down evidence that contradicts it.
- Create a positive, empowering alternative to each negative belief.

- Example: "I am constantly learning and growing" or "I have the creativity to find resources."

c. Doubt Dialogue:

- When you notice self-doubt creeping in, have a dialogue with it.
- Ask yourself: "Is this doubt based on fact or fear?"
- Respond to the doubt with your affirmations and reframed beliefs.

4. Success Visualization Scenario:

a. Choose a Specific Goal:

- Select one of your ambitious goals to focus on.

b. Write a Success Story:

- Write a detailed story as if you've already achieved this goal.
- Include the steps you took, obstacles you overcame, and how it feels to succeed.

c. Regular Reading:

- Read this success story every morning for a week.
- Allow yourself to fully immerse in the feelings of success.

5. Action Plan Development:

a. Break Down Your Goals:

- For each of your major goals, identify 3-5 key steps needed to achieve them.

b. Create a Timeline:

- Assign deadlines to each of these steps.

c. Daily Action:

- Identify one small action you can take each day towards your goals.
- Commit to taking this action, no matter how small.

6. Celebration and Reflection:

a. Celebrate Small Wins:

- At the end of each week, identify and celebrate the progress you've made towards your goals.
- Write down at least three achievements, no matter how small.
- Take a moment to feel genuine pride and gratitude for these accomplishments.

b. Reflection Journal:

- Keep a weekly reflection journal.
- Write about how your self-affirmations and visualizations are influencing your actions and mindset.

- Note any changes in your confidence levels or approach to challenges.

7. Accountability and Support:

a. Share Your Goals:

- Choose a trusted friend, family member, or mentor to share your goals with.
- Explain your visualization and affirmation practice to them.
- Ask them to check in with you regularly about your progress.

b. Visualization Partner:

- Find a partner who is also interested in this practice.
- Set up weekly calls to share your visualizations and affirmations.
- Offer each other encouragement and support.

8. Expanding Your Vision:

a. Monthly Vision Review:

- At the end of each month, review your goals and visualizations.
- Ask yourself: "Am I dreaming big enough?"
- Update your goals and visions as needed, always pushing yourself to believe in greater possibilities.

b. Inspiration Immersion:

- Regularly expose yourself to inspiring stories of others who have achieved similar goals.
- Read biographies, watch documentaries, or attend talks by successful individuals in your field.
- After each, reflect on how their journey reinforces your own belief in what's possible.

9. Overcoming Setbacks:

a. Setback Scenario Planning:

- For each of your major goals, imagine potential setbacks or obstacles.
- Visualize yourself overcoming these challenges with confidence and creativity.
- Write down specific strategies for dealing with each potential setback.

b. Resilience Affirmations:

- Develop a set of affirmations specifically focused on resilience and perseverance.
- Example: "I grow stronger with every challenge I face" or "Setbacks are opportunities for comeback."

10. Physical Embodiment:

a. Power Poses:

- Research and practice power poses that make you feel confident and capable.
- Hold these poses for two minutes before important meetings or events.

b. Visualization Walk:

- Take a daily walk while visualizing your success.
- Align your body language with the confidence of your future, successful self.

11. Gratitude Practice:

a. Daily Gratitude:

- Each night, write down three things you're grateful for.
- Include gratitude for your own qualities and actions that are moving you towards your goals.

b. Future Gratitude:

- Once a week, write a gratitude letter to your future self, thanking yourself for achieving your goals.

- Detail the positive impact these achievements have had on your life and others.

12. Belief Reinforcement:

a. Evidence Collection:

- Keep a running list of all evidence that supports your ability to achieve your goals.
- Include past successes, skills you've developed, obstacles you've overcome, and positive feedback you've received.

b. Belief Affirmation:

- Create a powerful statement that encapsulates your belief in your ability to achieve your goals.
- Repeat this statement to yourself whenever you face self-doubt or challenges.

Remember, the key to this exercise is consistency and genuine engagement. The more you practice these techniques, the more natural they will become, and the more impact they will have on your mindset and actions.

Believe in yourself and your goals with unwavering conviction. As you continue this practice, you'll likely find that your confidence grows, your goals become clearer, and opportunities begin to align with your vision. Remember, "You'll see it when you believe it." Your belief is the first step in turning your dreams into reality.

NOTES FROM CHAPTER 5:

CHAPTER 6

Cleaning Up the City

"We'll Figure It Out."

As our cleaning and staffing business continued to thrive, I found myself increasingly drawn to a larger mission. The contracts we were securing and the jobs we were creating were making a difference, but I couldn't shake the feeling that we could do more. Every day, as I drove through the streets of Detroit, I saw not just buildings that needed cleaning, but entire neighborhoods crying out for revitalization.

This realization sparked a new phase in our journey – one that would challenge us in ways we never expected, but also allow us to make an impact beyond our wildest dreams. We were about to embark on a mission to clean up not just individual buildings, but entire sections of our beloved city.

The idea came to me one morning as I was driving to a client meeting. I passed by a series of abandoned lots, overgrown with weeds and littered with trash. In that moment, my "Nature Smart" intelligence kicked in. Instead of seeing urban blight, I envisioned community gardens, green spaces that could provide fresh produce and a sense of pride to the neighborhood.

This vision was quickly followed by a cascade of ideas, my "Picture Smart" abilities painting a vivid image of what could be. I saw refurbished storefronts with local businesses thriving, streets lined with trees and flowers, and community centers buzzing with activity. It was a beautiful picture, but one that seemed almost impossibly far from the current reality.

But then I remembered one of our guiding principles: "We'll Figure It Out." We didn't need to have all the answers right away. We just needed to start, to take that first step, and trust in our ability to solve problems as they arose.

I called an emergency meeting with our leadership team that very afternoon. As I shared my vision, I could see a mix of excitement and apprehension on their faces. We were a cleaning and staffing company, after all. What did we know about urban renewal?

But as we discussed the idea, something remarkable happened. Each team member began to see how their unique skills and experiences could contribute to this larger mission. Our operations manager, who had a background in landscaping, got excited about the potential for green spaces. Our HR director saw an opportunity to create new job training programs. Our finance team started crunching numbers, looking for ways to make these projects economically sustainable.

It was a powerful reminder of another important ISM: "Every Second Counts." We couldn't afford to wait for someone else to solve these problems. Every day that passed was another day that our community suffered. We had the vision, we had the passion, and we had a team of dedicated individuals ready to make a difference. It was time to act.

Our first project was modest – cleaning up and converting one of those abandoned lots into a community garden. We partnered with a local nonprofit that had experience in urban agriculture, leveraging their expertise while providing the manpower and resources to make it happen.

The work was challenging. The lot was in worse shape than we initially realized, with contaminated soil that needed to be removed and replaced. We encountered red tape from city officials who were skeptical of our plans. And we faced resistance from some community members who had grown cynical after years of broken promises from would-be reformers.

But we persevered, guided by our belief that "We'll Figure It Out." When the soil contamination threatened to derail the project, we researched and implemented phytoremediation techniques, using plants to clean the soil naturally. When city officials dragged their feet on approvals, we engaged in a grassroots campaign to build community support and put pressure on the bureaucracy. And when community members expressed doubt, we invited them to be part of the process, incorporating their ideas and concerns into our plans.

Throughout this process, I found myself drawing heavily on my "Nature Smart" and "Picture Smart" abilities. My understanding of natural systems helped us design a garden that would be sustainable and productive, working with the local ecosystem rather than against it. And my ability to visualize and communicate our plans helped us win over skeptics, showing them not just what we wanted to do, but why it mattered.

After months of hard work, the garden was finally ready. The transformation was stunning. What had once been an eyesore was now a vibrant green space, with raised beds full of vegetables, fruit trees beginning to take root, and a small playground for neighborhood children.

But the physical transformation was just the beginning. We saw community members who had never spoken to each other working side by side in the garden. We saw children learning about nutrition and the environment. We saw elderly residents finding a new sense of purpose as they shared their gardening knowledge with younger generations.

The success of this first project gave us the confidence to think bigger. We began to look at other ways we could leverage our resources and expertise to make a difference in our community.

CHAPTER 6: CLEANING UP THE CITY

We expanded our vision from individual lots to entire blocks, and eventually to whole neighborhoods.

One of our most ambitious projects was the revitalization of a once-thriving commercial district that had fallen on hard times. Many of the storefronts were boarded up, and the few businesses that remained were struggling to survive. But where others saw decay, we saw potential.

We started by cleaning up the street, removing litter and graffiti, and planting trees along the sidewalks. Then, we began working with property owners to renovate the empty storefronts. We offered our cleaning and maintenance services at reduced rates to businesses willing to set up shop in the area. And we partnered with local artists to create murals and public art installations that celebrated the neighborhood's history and culture.

This project required us to think creatively about funding and sustainability. We couldn't rely solely on our own resources, so we had to find ways to make these initiatives self-sustaining. This is where the ISM "A Penny Saved Is A Penny" came into play. We looked for ways to maximize the impact of every dollar spent, and to create revenue streams that could support ongoing maintenance and development.

One innovative solution we came up with was a "community investment fund." We invited local residents and businesses to invest small amounts of money in specific revitalization projects. In return, they would receive a share of the revenue generated by these projects – whether it was rent from renovated properties or profits from community-owned businesses.

This approach not only provided us with additional funding but also gave community members a real stake in the success of these initiatives. It changed the dynamic from one of charity to one of partnership and shared ownership.

As our revitalization efforts gained momentum, we began to attract attention from city officials, other businesses, and even national media. People were fascinated by the idea of a cleaning company that had expanded its mission to include urban renewal and community development.

But with this attention came new challenges. Some accused us of gentrification, worried that our efforts would lead to rising property values and the displacement of long-time residents. Others questioned our motives, assuming that there must be some hidden profit motive behind our work.

These criticisms forced us to take a hard look at our methods and our goals. We realized that we needed to be more intentional about ensuring that our efforts benefited the existing community, not just attracted new investment. We doubled down on our commitment to creating jobs for local residents, supporting local businesses, and preserving the cultural heritage of the neighborhoods we were working in.

We also became more transparent about our financials, showing exactly how money was being spent and how profits (when there were any) were being reinvested in the community. We invited critics to join our planning sessions and incorporated their feedback into our projects.

Throughout all of this, our cleaning and staffing business continued to grow. In fact, our community revitalization work opened up new opportunities for our core business. As we cleaned up neighborhoods, demand for our services increased. As we renovated buildings, we secured new contracts. And as we created new green spaces, we were hired to maintain them.

But more importantly, we were creating a model for how businesses could be a force for positive change in their communities. We were demonstrating that it was possible to pursue profit and purpose simultaneously, and that by investing in our community, we were ultimately investing in our own success.

As our impact grew, so did our ambitions. We began to look at even larger-scale projects – converting abandoned factories into mixed-use developments, creating citywide networks of bike paths and green corridors, and developing innovative solutions for urban water management.

One project that I'm particularly proud of involved the transformation of an old, abandoned school building. Using my "Picture Smart" abilities, I envisioned turning this decaying structure into a community hub that would house a job training center, a health clinic, a daycare facility, and affordable housing units.

The project was enormously complex, requiring us to navigate zoning laws, secure historic preservation credits, and coordinate with multiple government agencies and nonprofit organizations. There were times when it seemed like the obstacles were insurmountable.

But every time we hit a roadblock, I reminded our team of our guiding principle: "We'll Figure It Out." And time and time again, we did. We found creative solutions to engineering challenges, developed innovative funding models, and built coalitions of support that helped us overcome political hurdles.

When the community hub finally opened its doors, it was a testament to what can be achieved when a group of dedicated individuals refuse to give up on their vision. The building that had once been a symbol of urban decay was now a beacon of hope and opportunity.

As our work continued, we began to see real, measurable impacts on the communities we were serving. Crime rates dropped in neighborhoods where we had created green spaces and community gardens. Local businesses reported increased revenue as the areas became more attractive to visitors. And perhaps most importantly, we saw a renewed sense of pride and ownership among residents.

But we also realized that true, lasting change required more than just physical transformation. It required a shift in mindset, a rekindling of hope, and the empowerment of community members to become agents of change themselves.

To this end, we started leadership development programs, teaching local residents the skills they needed to spearhead their own revitalization projects. We created mentorship programs that paired experienced professionals with aspiring entrepreneurs. And we worked with local schools to develop curricula that taught students about urban planning, environmental sustainability, and civic engagement.

Throughout all of this work, I continued to rely heavily on my "Nature Smart" and "Picture Smart" abilities. My understanding of natural systems helped us design projects that were environmentally sustainable and resilient. And my ability to visualize and communicate complex ideas helped us build support for our most ambitious initiatives.

As I reflect on our journey from a small cleaning company to a catalyst for urban renewal, I'm struck by how much of our success came down to our willingness to take on challenges that seemed beyond our capabilities. We didn't have all the answers when we started, but we had faith in our ability to figure things out as we went along.

This approach wasn't always easy. There were plenty of setbacks, mistakes, and moments of doubt along the way. But each challenge we overcame made us stronger and more capable. We learned to be adaptable, to think creatively, and to never lose sight of our ultimate goal – to make our city a better place for all its residents.

Our work is far from over. There are still neighborhoods in need of revitalization, still systemic issues that need to be addressed. But I'm more convinced than ever that with determination, creativity, and a willingness to roll up our sleeves and get to work, there's no problem we can't solve.

To all the aspiring change-makers out there, I say this: Don't wait for someone else to solve the problems in your community. You have unique skills, perspectives, and abilities that are needed. Trust in your capacity to figure things out as you go along. Remember that every second counts, and that even small actions can lead to big changes over time.

Your community needs you. Your city needs you. The world needs people who are willing to look at longstanding problems with fresh eyes and say, "We'll figure it out." So take that first step, whatever it may be. The journey of transforming your community starts with you.

Exercise: Brainstorm creative solutions to a problem in your community, leveraging your "Nature Smart" and "Picture Smart" abilities

This exercise is designed to help you tap into your "Nature Smart" and "Picture Smart" intelligences to develop innovative solutions for a problem in your community. By combining your understanding of natural systems with your ability to visualize and think spatially, you can come up with unique and effective ideas for positive change.

Step 1: Identify a Community Problem

Take some time to reflect on your community. What issues or challenges do you see? These could be environmental problems, social issues, or infrastructure needs. Choose one problem that you feel passionate about addressing.

Write down the problem in detail, considering its causes, effects, and who it impacts.

Step 2: Nature Smart Analysis

Now, let's apply your "Nature Smart" intelligence to this problem:

a) Natural Systems Parallel:

- Can you think of any natural systems or processes that might parallel this problem?
- How does nature deal with similar challenges?

b) Ecosystem Thinking:

- Consider the problem as part of a larger ecosystem. What other factors or systems is it connected to?
- How might changes in one area affect others?

c) Biomimicry:

- Are there any solutions in nature that could be adapted to address this problem?
- Think about how different plants or animals might solve a similar challenge.

Write down at least three insights or ideas that come from this nature-inspired analysis.

Step 3: Picture Smart Visualization

Now, let's engage your "Picture Smart" abilities:

a) Mental Imagery:

- Close your eyes and visualize your community as it is now, with the problem you've identified.
- Now, imagine your community with the problem solved. What does it look like? What has changed?

b) Spatial Relationships:

- Draw a simple map or diagram of the area affected by the problem.
- How could the space be reorganized or repurposed to address the issue?

c) Visual Metaphors:

- Can you think of a visual metaphor that represents either the problem or a potential solution?

- How might this metaphor inspire new ways of thinking about the issue?

Sketch out or describe in detail at least two visual concepts that emerged from this process.

Step 4: Combining Insights

Now, let's bring together the insights from your Nature Smart and Picture Smart analyses:

a) Review all the ideas and visualizations you've generated.

b) Look for connections or combinations that could lead to innovative solutions.

c) Develop at least three potential solutions that incorporate elements from both your nature-inspired and visually-inspired ideas.

Step 5: Refine and Elaborate

Choose the solution that you think has the most potential. Now, let's develop it further:

a) Implementation:

- How could this solution be implemented in your community?
- What resources would be needed?
- Who would need to be involved?

b) Impact:

- How would this solution address the original problem?
- What positive impacts might it have beyond the immediate issue?
- Are there any potential negative consequences to consider?

c) Visualization:

- Create a more detailed visualization of your solution. This could be a drawing, a map, a diagram, or even a simple model.
- Use this visual representation to help explain your idea to others.

Step 6: Action Plan

Finally, let's think about how to move this idea forward:

a) First Steps:

- What are the first three actions you could take to start implementing this solution?

b) Collaboration:

- Who in your community might be interested in or beneficial to this project?
- How could you present your idea to gain their support?

c) Learning and Iteration:

- What do you still need to learn to make this solution a reality?
- How could you test or pilot this idea on a small scale?

Remember, the goal of this exercise is not to develop a perfect, final solution, but to practice using your Nature Smart and Picture Smart abilities to approach community problems in creative ways. The process of brainstorming and visualizing solutions can often lead to unexpected insights and innovative approaches.

By combining your understanding of natural systems with your ability to think visually and spatially, you're tapping into powerful cognitive tools that can help you see problems and potential solutions in new ways. This kind of creative, interdisciplinary thinking is exactly what's needed to address the complex challenges facing our communities today.

Don't be afraid to think big or to propose ideas that might seem unconventional at first. Some of the most transformative solutions come from looking at old problems in new ways. And remember, just as in nature, the best solutions often emerge through a process of iteration and adaptation. Your initial idea is just the seed – with nurturing and refinement, it has the potential to grow into something truly impactful for your community.

NOTES FROM CHAPTER 6:

CHAPTER 7

Keys to the City

"Numbers And Money Follow; They Do Not Lead."

As our cleaning business expanded and our community revitalization efforts gained momentum, I found myself in a position I never could have imagined when I was living out of my van just a few years earlier. We were now a major employer in Detroit, with contracts spanning across the city and beyond. Our urban renewal projects were being hailed as models for community-driven development. And, yes, the financial success had followed.

But with this success came new challenges and responsibilities. As our influence grew, so did the pressure to focus on the bottom line, to prioritize profits over purpose. It was during this time that I found myself returning again and again to one of our core ISMs: "Numbers And Money Follow; They Do Not Lead."

This principle had guided us from the beginning, but now it was being put to the test. We were at a crossroads, facing decisions that would define not just the future of our business, but our role in the community and our legacy as an organization.

I remember sitting in my office late one night, poring over financial reports and growth projections. The numbers were impressive, showing steady growth and healthy profits. But as I looked at these figures, I felt a sense of unease. Something was missing.

That's when it hit me - these numbers, as important as they were, didn't tell the whole story. They didn't capture the sense of pride I saw in our employees' eyes when they transformed a blighted lot into a community garden. They didn't reflect the joy of a single mother who, through our job training program, was able to secure stable employment for the first time in years. They didn't measure the renewed sense of hope that was palpable in the neighborhoods we were working in.

I realized that if we let these numbers lead us, if we made decisions solely based on financial metrics, we risked losing sight of why we started this journey in the first place. Our purpose wasn't to make money; it was to make a difference. The money was a means to an end, not the end itself.

This realization led to a renewed commitment to prioritizing purpose over profits. We made a conscious decision to evaluate every opportunity, every project, and every partnership not just in terms of its financial potential, but its alignment with our mission and its potential impact on the community.

This wasn't always an easy path to follow. There were times when we turned down lucrative contracts because they didn't align with our values. We invested in community projects that didn't have an immediate financial return but that we believed would have a lasting positive impact. We prioritized hiring and training local residents, even when it would have been cheaper and easier to bring in workers from outside the community.

But time and time again, we found that when we stayed true to our purpose, the numbers followed. Our commitment to the community built trust and loyalty, leading to new opportunities and partnerships. Our investment in our employees resulted in higher productivity and lower turnover. Our focus on sustainable, community-driven development attracted socially conscious investors and clients who shared our values.

As we navigated this path, I found myself drawing on another important ISM: "We Eat Our Own Dog Food." This principle reminded us to live by the values and practices we espoused. If we were going to talk about the importance of community investment, we needed to be actively investing in our community. If we were going to promote sustainable practices, we needed to ensure our own operations were environmentally responsible.

This commitment to authenticity became a powerful driver of innovation and growth. For example, when we talked about the importance of local hiring, we didn't just set hiring targets - we created comprehensive job training and support programs to ensure local residents had the skills and resources they needed to succeed. When we promoted green spaces, we didn't just build parks - we integrated green design principles into all of our projects, from our office buildings to our cleaning practices.

Living our values in this way not only strengthened our impact but also created a powerful sense of alignment within our organization. Our employees knew that we weren't just paying lip service to these ideas - we were putting them into practice every day. This built a culture of authenticity and commitment that became one of our greatest assets.

As our influence in the city grew, I found myself being invited to more high-level meetings and events. City officials wanted our input on development plans. Other business leaders sought our advice on community engagement. We were even asked to consult on urban renewal projects in other cities.

It was flattering, and at times, a bit overwhelming. I, a former homeless man with no formal business education, was now being treated as a key player in Detroit's revitalization. There were moments when the impostor syndrome threatened to creep back in, when I wondered if I really belonged in these rooms with powerful politicians and wealthy executives.

But in those moments, I reminded myself of where I came from and why I was doing this work. I wasn't there because of my pedigree or my connections. I was there because of the impact we had made, the trust we had built in the community, and the vision we had for a better Detroit.

I made a conscious effort to stay grounded, to never forget my roots. I continued to spend time in the neighborhoods we were working in, talking to residents, listening to their concerns and ideas. I made sure that even as our company grew, we maintained a connection to the day-to-day realities of the communities we served.

This commitment to staying connected to our roots became a key part of our leadership philosophy. We instituted a policy that all of our executives, regardless of their position, would spend time each month working alongside our cleaning crews or volunteering in our community projects. This not only kept us humble and in touch with the realities of our work, but it also fostered a sense of solidarity and shared purpose throughout the organization.

As we continued to grow and evolve, I found myself drawing more and more on my "Music Smart" intelligence. This might seem like an odd fit for a cleaning and urban development business, but I found that my understanding of rhythm, harmony, and composition was incredibly valuable in creating a sense of balance and flow in our work.

I began to think of our various projects and initiatives as different instruments in an orchestra. Each had its own unique sound and role, but they needed to work together in harmony to create something truly beautiful. Our cleaning contracts provided a steady rhythm, the foundation upon which everything else was built. Our job training programs added a melodic line, creating opportunities for individual growth and development. Our urban renewal projects were like bold, sweeping crescendos, transforming entire neighborhoods.

This musical metaphor helped us think more holistically about our work. We weren't just a collection of separate projects or departments - we were creating a symphony of change in our city. This perspective allowed us to better coordinate our efforts, to ensure that each initiative complemented and enhanced the others.

I also applied this musical thinking to our organizational culture. Just as a great piece of music has moments of intensity and moments of calm, I recognized the need for balance in our work. We implemented policies to ensure that our employees had time for rest and rejuvenation, understanding that this was essential for sustained, high-quality performance.

We created rhythms in our work - daily check-ins, weekly team meetings, monthly community events - that provided a sense of structure and continuity. But within this structure, we also allowed for improvisation and creativity, encouraging our team members to bring their unique talents and perspectives to their work.

This approach created a workplace that was both highly productive and deeply fulfilling. Our employees weren't just going through the motions - they were active participants in creating something meaningful and beautiful.

CHAPTER 7: KEYS TO THE CITY

As our influence grew, we began to see opportunities to shape policy and drive larger-scale change in the city. We were invited to participate in task forces and committees focused on issues like affordable housing, workforce development, and environmental sustainability.

At first, I was hesitant to enter this more political arena. I worried that getting involved in policy discussions might distract us from our on-the-ground work or compromise our independence. But I soon realized that if we wanted to create lasting change, we needed to engage with the systems and structures that shaped our city.

We approached this new challenge with the same principles that had guided us from the beginning. We focused on purpose over politics, on creating real impact rather than scoring political points. We used our firsthand experience and data from our projects to advocate for policies that would support community-driven development and create opportunities for marginalized residents.

Our unique perspective - as a business that was deeply embedded in the community - allowed us to bridge gaps between different stakeholders. We could speak the language of business, explaining to other companies how investing in the community could benefit their bottom line. But we could also authentically represent the needs and aspirations of community members, ensuring their voices were heard in discussions about the future of the city.

This work wasn't always easy. We faced pushback from those who were invested in maintaining the status quo. We had to navigate complex political dynamics and competing interests. But we stayed true to our purpose, always asking ourselves, "What will have the greatest positive impact for our community?"

Throughout this journey, I never lost sight of the fact that our success - financial and otherwise - was built on the trust and support of our community. We made it a priority to continually reinvest in the neighborhoods we served, not just through our official projects, but through a myriad of small, everyday actions.

We sponsored local sports teams and community events. We provided free cleaning services to schools and community centers. We created a microloan program to help local residents start small businesses. We saw these investments not as charity, but as an integral part of building a thriving, sustainable community ecosystem.

As I reflect on our journey - from a small cleaning operation to a catalyst for citywide change - I'm struck by how much of our success came from staying true to our core values and purpose. By prioritizing impact over profit, by living our values authentically, by staying connected to our roots, and by approaching our work with creativity and a sense of harmony, we were able to create something far greater than I ever could have imagined.

The keys to the city, I've learned, are not found in wealth or political power. They're found in the trust of the community, in the ability to bring people together around a shared vision, and in the commitment to creating value for others. When you focus on these things, the numbers and the money do indeed follow.

To all the aspiring entrepreneurs and change-makers out there, I say this: Don't let the pursuit of profit distract you from your true purpose. Stay true to your values, even when it's difficult. Stay connected to the people and communities you serve. And always remember that your work is part of a larger symphony of change. Play your part with passion, with purpose, and with a commitment to creating harmony in the world around you.

Your unique talents, your experiences, and your vision are needed. The world is waiting for the music only you can create. So tune your instrument, find your rhythm, and play your heart out. The most beautiful symphonies often start with a single, brave note.

Exercise: Identify your core values and purpose, and ensure that they align with your business goals and decisions

This exercise is designed to help you clarify your core values and purpose, and to ensure that these fundamental principles are aligned with your business goals and decision-making processes. By the end of this exercise, you should have a clearer understanding of what truly drives you and how to integrate these values into your professional life.

1. Core Values Identification:

a) Value Brainstorming:

- Take 10 minutes to write down all the values that are important to you. Don't censor yourself; write down everything that comes to mind.

- Examples might include: integrity, innovation, sustainability, community, excellence, empathy, etc.

b) Value Prioritization:

- Review your list and circle the 10 values that resonate most strongly with you.
- From these 10, narrow it down to your top 5 core values.

c) Value Definition:

- For each of your top 5 values, write a brief definition of what this value means to you.
- Example: Integrity - Always doing the right thing, even when no one is watching.

2. Purpose Statement Development:

a) Reflection Questions:

Answer the following questions:

- What are you passionate about?
- What unique skills or perspectives do you bring to the world?
- What problems do you want to solve?
- How do you want to make a difference in people's lives?

b) Purpose Statement Draft:

Based on your answers, write a draft purpose statement. This should be a concise statement that captures why you do what you do.

Example: "My purpose is to use sustainable business practices to create economic opportunities in underserved communities."

c) Refinement:

- Share your draft statement with a trusted friend or mentor for feedback.
- Refine your statement based on this feedback and your own reflection.

3. Business Goal Alignment:

a) Current Goal Listing:

- Write down your current top 3-5 business goals.

b) Value Alignment Check:

- For each goal, ask yourself: "How does this goal align with my core values and purpose?"
- If there's misalignment, how can the goal be adjusted to better reflect your values and purpose?

c) Purpose-Driven Goal Setting:

- Based on your purpose statement, what new goals or initiatives should you consider?
- Add these to your list of business goals.

4. Decision-Making Framework:

a) Recent Decision Analysis:

- Think of 3-5 significant business decisions you've made recently.
- For each decision, evaluate how well it aligned with your core values and purpose.

b) Future Decision Framework:

- Create a set of questions based on your values and purpose to guide future decisions.
- Example: "Does this decision support our commitment to sustainability?" "How will this impact our community?"

c) Value-Based Scenario Planning:

- Imagine 2-3 potential future scenarios your business might face.
- Use your values and purpose to guide how you would approach each scenario.

5. Organizational Integration:

a) Communication Plan:

- Develop a plan to communicate your core values and purpose to your team, customers, and other stakeholders.

- How can you make these principles visible in your day-to-day operations?

b) Policy Review:

- Review your current business policies and practices.
- Identify areas where changes could be made to better reflect your values and purpose.

c) Culture Building:

- Brainstorm ways to reinforce your values and purpose in your organizational culture.
- This might include recognition programs, team-building activities, or changes to your hiring practices.

6. Measurement and Accountability:

a) Impact Metrics:

- Develop 3-5 key metrics that will help you measure how well you're living up to your values and purpose.
- These might include both quantitative and qualitative measures.

b) Regular Review:

- Set up a system for regularly reviewing your alignment with your values and purpose.

- This could be a monthly personal reflection, quarterly team reviews, or annual stakeholder surveys.

c) Accountability Partners:

- Identify 1-2 people who can serve as accountability partners, helping you stay true to your values and purpose.
- Set up regular check-ins with these partners.

7. Personal Development Plan:

a) Skill Gap Analysis:

- Based on your values and purpose, are there skills you need to develop to be more effective?
- Create a plan to acquire or improve these skills.

b) Learning Agenda:

- Identify books, courses, or experiences that can deepen your understanding and application of your core values.

c) Mentorship:

- Consider seeking a mentor who embodies the values and purpose you aspire to.
- If you're in a position to do so, consider how you can mentor others in living their values.

8. Reflection and Iteration:

a) Journal:

- Start a journal to regularly reflect on how you're living your values and purpose in your business.
- Note successes, challenges, and insights.

b) Annual Review:

- Set aside time each year to review and potentially refine your values, purpose, and goals.
- How have they evolved? Are they still serving you and your business well?

c) Continuous Improvement:

- Based on your reflections, what one thing can you commit to improving in the coming month to better align your business with your values and purpose?

Remember, aligning your business with your core values and purpose is an ongoing process. It requires constant attention, reflection, and sometimes difficult choices. But by staying true to what you believe in and why you do what you do, you create a foundation for meaningful success and lasting impact.

This alignment not only leads to more fulfilling work but often results in better business outcomes as well. When your actions consistently reflect your values, you build trust with your team, your customers, and your community. This trust becomes a powerful asset, opening doors to new opportunities and helping you navigate challenges.

Moreover, by clearly articulating and living your values and purpose, you attract like-minded individuals - both employees and customers - who resonate with your mission. This creates a virtuous cycle, where your impact grows and your ability to stay true to your values strengthens.

Remember, in the words of the ISM we've been discussing, "Numbers And Money Follow; They Do Not Lead." By putting your values and purpose at the forefront of your business decisions, you set the stage for success that goes beyond financial metrics - success that makes a real difference in the world and leaves a lasting legacy.

NOTES FROM CHAPTER 7:

CHAPTER 8

The Future is Bright

"Innovation Is Rewarded. Execution Is Worshipped."

As I sit in my office, looking out over the Detroit skyline, I can't help but marvel at the journey that has brought us here. From a single man with a mop and a dream to a company that has helped reshape the landscape of our beloved city, both literally and figuratively. The path has been far from straight or easy, but it has been incredibly rewarding.

Our success has been built on a foundation of hard work, perseverance, and an unwavering commitment to our values. But as we look to the future, I'm reminded of another crucial ISM that has guided us: "Innovation Is Rewarded. Execution Is Worshipped." This principle has been at the heart of our growth and will continue to drive us forward as we face new challenges and opportunities.

Innovation has been a constant thread throughout our journey. From the early days when we reimagined what a cleaning company could be, to our forays into urban renewal and community development, we've always sought new and better ways to serve our clients and our community. But we've also learned that innovation alone is not enough. It's the execution - the ability to turn ideas into reality - that truly sets us apart.

As we look to the future, we see a world full of challenges that need innovative solutions. Climate change, urbanization, inequality - these are issues that will require new thinking and bold action. But they also present opportunities for those willing to step up and make a difference.

We're already working on several exciting initiatives that embody this spirit of innovation and execution. One of our most ambitious projects is a citywide green infrastructure program. We're partnering with environmental engineers and urban planners to develop a network of rain gardens, bioswales, and permeable pavements that will help manage stormwater runoff, reduce pollution, and create beautiful, functional green spaces throughout the city.

This project is a perfect example of how we're applying our "Nature Smart" intelligence on a larger scale. We're not just cleaning up the city; we're working with natural systems to create sustainable, resilient urban environments. And we're executing this vision block by block, neighborhood by neighborhood, turning innovative ideas into tangible improvements in people's lives.

Another area where we're pushing the boundaries of innovation is in our cleaning technologies. We're developing new, eco-friendly cleaning solutions that are not only more effective but also better for the environment and safer for our workers. We're also exploring the use of robotics and AI to enhance our cleaning processes, allowing our human workers to focus on higher-value tasks that require creativity and problem-solving skills.

But as excited as we are about these technological innovations, we never lose sight of the human element. We're constantly looking for ways to innovate in our training and development programs, ensuring that our workforce has the skills and support they need to thrive in an ever-changing job market.

One program I'm particularly proud of is our "Future Leaders" initiative. We identify employees at all levels of the organization who show leadership potential, regardless of their current position or background. We then provide them with intensive training in business management, community development, and sustainable practices. The goal is to create a pipeline of leaders who understand our values and have the skills to drive our mission forward.

This focus on developing our people is a key part of our execution strategy. We know that even the most innovative ideas are only as good as the people implementing them. By investing in our workforce, we're ensuring that we have the capacity to execute on our ambitious plans.

As we pursue these innovations, we're guided by another crucial ISM: "Do The Right Thing." This principle is at the core of everything we do. It means making decisions based on what's best for our employees, our community, and our planet, even when it might not be the easiest or most profitable choice in the short term.

For example, as we've grown and become more successful, we've had opportunities to expand rapidly into other cities. While this could have led to quick profits, we've chosen to grow more slowly and sustainably. We want to ensure that as we expand, we're able to maintain the same level of community engagement and positive impact that has defined our work in Detroit.

We've also made a commitment to transparency and ethical business practices that go beyond what's required by law. We publish detailed reports on our social and environmental impact, openly share our successes and failures, and actively seek feedback from our employees and community members. This commitment to doing the right thing has earned us trust and respect, which we believe is far more valuable than any short-term financial gain.

As I reflect on our journey and look to the future, I'm filled with a sense of excitement and possibility. But I'm also acutely aware of the responsibility we bear. Our success has given us a platform and a voice, and we intend to use it to advocate for positive change on a broader scale.

We're increasingly involved in policy discussions at the local, state, and even national level. We're sharing our experiences and insights to help shape policies that support sustainable urban development, create economic opportunities in underserved communities, and promote environmental stewardship.

But even as we engage with these larger issues, we remain committed to the principle of simplicity. We've found that often, the most effective solutions are the simplest ones. This doesn't mean they're easy to implement - far from it. But by focusing on fundamental principles and clear goals, we're able to cut through complexity and achieve meaningful results.

This commitment to simplicity is reflected in our approach to problem-solving. When faced with a challenge, we always start by asking, "What's the simplest way we could address this?" Often, this leads us to solutions that are not only more effective but also more sustainable and scalable.

As we continue to grow and evolve, I'm more convinced than ever of the importance of nurturing and developing one's Genius-level Talent. Each of us has unique gifts and abilities that, when recognized and cultivated, can lead to extraordinary achievements.

My own journey has been a testament to this. My "Nature Smart" and "Picture Smart" abilities, combined with my "People Smart" intelligence, have allowed me to see possibilities where others saw only problems. They've enabled me to envision a better future for our city and to inspire others to work towards that vision.

But I'm also aware that my talents alone were not enough. It was the combination of these abilities with hard work, perseverance, and a willingness to learn and adapt that allowed us to achieve what we have. And crucially, it was the recognition that my talents were

131

most powerful when combined with the diverse abilities of our team members.

That's why we put so much emphasis on helping our employees discover and develop their own Genius-level Talents. We believe that when people are operating in alignment with their unique abilities, they're not only more productive and fulfilled, but they're also able to contribute in ways that can truly change the world.

We've developed a comprehensive program to help our employees identify and nurture their Genius-level Talents. This includes assessments to help people understand their natural strengths, mentoring programs that pair employees with others who share similar abilities, and opportunities to apply these talents in new and challenging contexts.

The results have been remarkable. We've seen employees discover passions and abilities they never knew they had. We've watched as people who once felt stuck in dead-end jobs have blossomed into innovative problem-solvers and inspiring leaders. And we've benefited as a company from the incredible diversity of talents and perspectives that this approach has fostered.

As we look to the future, I'm filled with optimism. Not because I think the challenges ahead will be easy - they won't be. But because I believe in the power of human ingenuity and determination. I believe in the potential of every individual to make a difference. And I believe that when we come together, guided by strong values and a shared purpose, there's no limit to what we can achieve.

CHAPTER 8: THE FUTURE IS BRIGHT

To all the readers of this book, I want to offer a challenge and an encouragement. The challenge is this: Discover your own Genius-level Talent. Take the time to reflect on your unique abilities, the things that come naturally to you, the areas where you excel without even trying. These are clues to your Genius-level Talent.

But don't stop at discovery. Nurture these talents. Develop them. Find ways to apply them in your work and in your community. Because the world needs your unique gifts. We face challenges that will require all of our collective intelligence and creativity to solve. Your Genius-level Talent, whatever it may be, is part of the solution.

And here's the encouragement: The future is bright. Yes, we face significant challenges. But we also have unprecedented opportunities to make a positive impact. We have technologies and resources that previous generations could only dream of. We have a growing awareness of the interconnectedness of our world and the need for sustainable, equitable solutions.

Most importantly, we have each other. We have the collective intelligence and creativity of billions of people, each with their own Genius-level Talents. When we come together, guided by strong values and a commitment to doing the right thing, there's no challenge we can't overcome, no problem we can't solve.

As we close this chapter and look to the future, let's remember the ISM that has brought us this far: "Innovation Is Rewarded. Execution Is Worshipped." Let's continue to push the boundaries of what's possible, to dream big and think creatively. But let's also roll up our sleeves and do the hard work of turning those dreams into reality.

Let's commit to doing the right thing, even when it's difficult. Let's strive for simplicity in our solutions, even as we tackle complex problems. And let's never forget the power of our individual and collective Genius-level Talents to create positive change in the world.

The future is bright, not because it will be easy, but because we have the power to shape it. So let's get to work. The world is waiting for the unique contribution that only you can make. The time to start is now.

Exercise: Identify your Genius-level Talent and brainstorm ways to develop and apply it in your personal and professional life

This exercise is designed to help you discover, nurture, and apply your Genius-level Talent. Remember, your Genius-level Talent is more than just something you're good at - it's a unique combination of abilities that allows you to excel in ways that others might find difficult or impossible. Let's begin:

1. Self-Reflection:

Take some time to reflect on the following questions. Write down your answers in detail:

a) What activities do you find yourself naturally drawn to?

b) What tasks or challenges do you find easy, that others seem to struggle with?

c) When do you feel most "in the zone" or lose track of time because you're so engrossed in what you're doing?

d) What kinds of problems do people often come to you for help with?

e) What were you particularly good at or interested in as a child?

f) What do others often compliment you on or recognize you for?

2. Multiple Intelligences Assessment:

Based on Howard Gardner's theory of multiple intelligences, rate yourself on a scale of 1-10 in each of these areas:

- Linguistic (Word Smart)
- Logical-Mathematical (Number/Reasoning Smart)
- Spatial (Picture Smart)
- Musical (Music Smart)
- Bodily-Kinesthetic (Body Smart)
- Interpersonal (People Smart)
- Intrapersonal (Self Smart)
- Naturalistic (Nature Smart)
- Existential (Life Smart)

Identify your top 2-3 intelligences. How do these align with your reflections from step 1?

3. Feedback Collection:

Reach out to 5-10 people who know you well (family, friends, colleagues) and ask them:

a) What do they think you're particularly good at?

b) When have they seen you at your best?

c) What unique qualities or abilities do they think you bring to your work or relationships?

Look for patterns or themes in their responses.

4. Peak Experiences Analysis:

Think about 3-5 times in your life when you felt particularly successful or fulfilled. For each experience:

a) What were you doing?

b) What skills or abilities were you using?

c) What about the experience made it so positive for you?

Look for common elements across these experiences.

5. Synthesis:

Based on your reflections, the multiple intelligences assessment, feedback from others, and analysis of your peak experiences, try to articulate your Genius-level Talent. This might be a combination of specific skills, intelligences, and personal qualities.

Write a paragraph describing your Genius-level Talent. Remember, this is unique to you - it's not just a list of skills, but a description of how you uniquely approach and excel at certain types of tasks or challenges.

6. Development Plan:

Now that you've identified your Genius-level Talent, let's create a plan to develop it further:

a) Learning: What books, courses, or experiences could help you deepen your knowledge or skills in areas related to your Genius-level Talent?

b) Practice: What activities could you engage in regularly to practice and strengthen your Genius-level Talent?

c) Mentorship: Who could serve as a mentor to help you develop your Genius-level Talent further? This might be someone who has a similar talent or who excels in a field where your talent could be applied.

d) Stretch Goals: What's a challenging goal you could set that would require you to really leverage and grow your Genius-level Talent?

7. Application in Personal Life:

Brainstorm at least 5 ways you could apply your Genius-level Talent in your personal life. These could be related to hobbies, relationships, personal growth, or community involvement.

8. Application in Professional Life:

a) Current Role: How could you apply your Genius-level Talent more fully in your current job or business? List at least 3 specific ways.

b) Career Development: How might your Genius-level Talent guide your future career choices? Are there roles or fields where your talent would be particularly valuable?

c) Entrepreneurial Opportunities: Could your Genius-level Talent form the basis of a new business or side project? Brainstorm 2-3 possibilities.

9. Value Creation:

Reflect on how your Genius-level Talent could create value for others:

a) How could it help solve problems in your community or industry?

b) How could it contribute to causes or issues you care about?

c) How could it enhance the work of a team or organization?

10. Action Plan:

Based on your reflections and ideas from steps 6-9, create a 30-day action plan to start developing and applying your Genius-level Talent more intentionally. Include specific, measurable actions you'll take each week.

11. Accountability:

Share your Genius-level Talent description and your 30-day plan with a trusted friend, family member, or colleague. Ask them to check in with you regularly on your progress.

12. Reflection and Iteration:

After 30 days, reflect on your experiences:

a) What successes did you have in developing and applying your Genius-level Talent?

b) What challenges did you face?

c) How has your understanding of your Genius-level Talent evolved?

d) What will you do differently in the next 30 days?

Remember, discovering and developing your Genius-level Talent is an ongoing process. Be patient with yourself, stay curious, and remain open to new possibilities. Your Genius-level Talent may evolve and reveal new facets over time.

The key is to stay attuned to what energizes you, what you excel at, and where you can create the most value. As you continue to develop and apply your Genius-level Talent, you'll likely find that your work becomes more fulfilling, your impact grows, and new opportunities open up.

Embrace this journey of self-discovery and growth. Your Genius-level Talent is a gift - to yourself and to the world. By nurturing it and applying it purposefully, you can create a life and career that is truly extraordinary, and make a unique contribution that only you can make.

Remember the ISM we discussed: "Innovation Is Rewarded. Execution Is Worshipped." As you develop your Genius-level Talent, look for innovative ways to apply it. But don't stop at ideas - put them into action. It's in the execution, in the consistent application of your unique abilities, that you'll create real value and make a lasting impact.

The future is bright, and your Genius-level Talent is part of that brightness. Nurture it, apply it, and watch as it illuminates not just your own path, but the paths of those around you. The world is waiting for the unique light that only you can bring. So shine brightly, and light the way for others to follow.

NOTES FROM CHAPTER 8:

CONCLUSION

"The Packaging Is Just As Important As The Contents"

As we come to the end of this journey together, I'm reminded of an important lesson I learned early on in my entrepreneurial career: "The Packaging Is Just As Important As The Contents." This ISM has been a guiding principle not just in how we present our services or products, but in how we communicate our story, our values, and our vision to the world.

Throughout this book, I've shared with you the raw, unvarnished truth of my journey - from homelessness to building a multimillion-dollar business that's changing lives and revitalizing communities. But the power of this story doesn't lie just in the events themselves. It lies in how we tell it, how we package it in a way that resonates with others and inspires them to action.

This principle of packaging is about more than just making things look good on the surface. It's about understanding that how we present our ideas, our visions, and ourselves is integral to their success. It's about recognizing that inspiration and motivation are just as crucial as information and instruction.

As I reflect on the key takeaways and lessons from my journey, I realize that each one is both a piece of content - a lesson learned, a principle followed - and a package - a story that brings that lesson to life and makes it relatable and actionable for others.

Let's revisit some of these key takeaways:

1. "The Inches We Need Are Everywhere Around Us": This lesson taught us to look for opportunities in unexpected places, to see potential where others see problems. The content of this lesson is about opportunity recognition, but the packaging is the story of how a homeless man saw the potential in a simple cleaning job and turned it into a thriving business.

2. "Every Client. Every Time. No Exceptions. No Excuses.": This principle emphasizes the importance of consistent, high-quality service. But it's packaged in the stories of how we went above and beyond for our clients, even when it was difficult or inconvenient, and how this dedication led to our growth and success.

3. "We'll Figure It Out": This lesson is about resourcefulness and problem-solving. But it's packaged in the numerous stories of how we faced seemingly insurmountable challenges and found creative solutions, from dealing with contaminated soil in our first community garden to navigating complex regulations in our urban renewal projects.

4. "Numbers And Money Follow; They Do Not Lead": This principle reminds us to prioritize purpose over profits. It's packaged

in the stories of how we made difficult decisions that prioritized community impact over short-term financial gain, and how this approach ultimately led to greater success and fulfillment.

5. "Innovation Is Rewarded. Execution Is Worshipped": This lesson emphasizes the importance of not just having good ideas, but bringing them to life. It's packaged in the stories of our various innovative projects and how we worked tirelessly to turn these ideas into reality.

Each of these lessons, and indeed every story shared in this book, is a testament to the power of effective packaging. By presenting these lessons through personal stories, vivid examples, and relatable experiences, we've aimed to make them more than just abstract principles. We've tried to make them come alive, to make them feel real and achievable for you, the reader.

This brings us to one of the most crucial lessons of all - the importance of effectively communicating your story and inspiring others. Your journey, your struggles, your triumphs - these are not just events that happened to you. They are powerful tools for connection, inspiration, and change.

When we share our stories authentically and passionately, we create connections. We show others that they're not alone in their struggles, that success is possible even in the face of seemingly insurmountable odds. We inspire hope, ignite imagination, and motivate action.

But effective storytelling is about more than just recounting events. It's about finding the universal themes in our personal experiences. It's about packaging our journey in a way that others can see themselves in it, can draw lessons from it, can be inspired by it.

This is why, throughout this book, I've tried to balance the specific details of my experiences with broader insights and principles that you can apply to your own life and business. I've shared not just what happened, but why it mattered, what I learned from it, and how you might apply these lessons in your own context.

Now, as we conclude this book, I want to issue a call to action. The stories and lessons shared here are not meant to simply be read and forgotten. They are meant to be lived, to be applied, to be the catalyst for your own journey of growth and impact.

I challenge you to take these principles - the ISMs we've discussed, the lessons we've explored - and apply them in your own life and business. But don't just apply them blindly. Package them in a way that resonates with your own experiences, your own vision, your own voice.

Remember, your story is unique. Your experiences, your struggles, your triumphs - they are yours alone. But the lessons you've learned, the insights you've gained, these have the power to inspire and guide others. Don't underestimate the power of your story, properly packaged and passionately shared.

As you move forward on your own entrepreneurial journey, I encourage you to embrace the power of combining passion and Genius-level Talent to find your purpose. This combination is potent. Your passion fuels your perseverance, drives you to push through challenges and setbacks. Your Genius-level Talent gives you a unique edge, a special way of seeing and doing that sets you apart.

When you align your passion with your Genius-level Talent, and direct them towards a purpose greater than yourself, you create a force for change that is truly unstoppable. This alignment is what allowed me to turn a simple cleaning job into a vehicle for community transformation. It's what can allow you to turn your own skills and experiences into a force for positive change in your own sphere of influence.

But remember, identifying your passion and Genius-level Talent is just the first step. The real magic happens in how you package and present them to the world. How will you communicate your vision in a way that inspires others to join you? How will you present your ideas in a way that makes others sit up and take notice? How will you tell your story in a way that motivates others to write new chapters in their own stories?

These are the questions that will determine the impact of your journey. Because in the end, true success isn't just about what you achieve for yourself. It's about how you inspire and empower others to achieve their own dreams.

As we close this book, I want to leave you with a final thought. The journey of entrepreneurship, of making a difference in the world, is not an easy one. There will be setbacks, doubts, and moments of fear. But remember this: every challenge you face, every obstacle you overcome, is not just a part of your journey. It's a part of your story. It's content waiting to be packaged in a way that can inspire and guide others.

So embrace every part of your journey - the highs and the lows, the victories and the setbacks. See them all as material for the story you're writing with your life. And commit to packaging that story in a way that not only reflects your truth but also ignites the potential in others.

Your story matters. Your vision matters. Your passion and your Genius-level Talent matter. The world is waiting for the unique contribution that only you can make. So go forth, write your story, and package it in a way that changes lives and transforms communities. The future is bright, and you have the power to make it even brighter.

Exercise: Create an action plan to implement the lessons learned from the book in your own entrepreneurial journey

This exercise is designed to help you translate the insights and principles from this book into concrete actions in your own life and business. Remember, the true value of any learning comes not just from understanding, but from application. Let's begin:

1. Personal Reflection:

Take some time to reflect on the key lessons from the book that resonated most strongly with you. Write down:

a) Three ISMs or principles that you found most inspiring or relevant to your situation.

b) Two stories or examples from the book that particularly moved you or made you think differently about your own journey.

c) One major insight about yourself or your approach to business that you gained from reading this book.

2. Vision Crafting:

Based on what you've learned and your own aspirations:

a) Write a brief description of where you want to be in your entrepreneurial journey five years from now. Be as specific and vivid as possible.

b) Identify three major goals you want to achieve in the next year that will move you closer to this vision.

3. Opportunity Identification:

Applying the principle "The Inches We Need Are Everywhere Around Us":

a) List five overlooked opportunities or untapped resources in your current environment that you could potentially leverage.

b) For each opportunity, brainstorm two ways you could take advantage of it, no matter how small or seemingly insignificant.

4. Service Excellence Plan:

Embracing "Every Client. Every Time. No Exceptions. No Excuses.":

a) Identify three ways you can improve your current level of service or product quality.

b) Develop a system for consistently gathering and acting on feedback from your clients or customers.

5. Problem-Solving Approach:

Adopting the "We'll Figure It Out" mentality:

a) List three current challenges or obstacles in your business or entrepreneurial journey.

b) For each challenge, brainstorm five potential solutions, no matter how unconventional they might seem.

c) Choose one challenge and create a step-by-step plan to implement your best solution.

6. Purpose-Driven Decision Making:

Applying "Numbers And Money Follow; They Do Not Lead":

a) Clearly articulate your core purpose or mission beyond making money.

b) Identify three decisions you need to make in your business. For each decision, write down how you will ensure it aligns with your core purpose.

7. Innovation and Execution:

Embracing "Innovation Is Rewarded. Execution Is Worshipped":

a) Brainstorm five innovative ideas that could improve your business or solve a problem in your industry.

b) Choose the most promising idea and create a detailed execution plan, including timelines and required resources.

8. Genius-level Talent Application:

Based on the Genius-level Talent you identified in the previous exercise:

a) List three ways you can more fully leverage your Genius-level Talent in your current business or entrepreneurial pursuits.

b) Identify one new project or initiative you could start that would allow you to fully utilize your Genius-level Talent.

9. Story Packaging:

Applying "The Packaging Is Just As Important As The Contents":

a) Write down your entrepreneurial story in a compelling way, highlighting your unique journey, challenges overcome, and lessons learned.

b) Identify three key messages or lessons from your story that could inspire or guide others.

c) Brainstorm three different ways you could share your story (e.g., blog posts, speaking engagements, mentoring).

10. Network and Community Building:

Recognizing the importance of connections and support:

a) Identify five individuals or organizations in your industry or community who could be valuable connections.

b) Develop a plan to reach out to these contacts and build meaningful relationships.

c) Think of three ways you could give back to your community or industry, applying the lessons you've learned.

11. Continuous Learning Plan:

Committing to ongoing growth and development:

a) List three skills you need to develop to achieve your entrepreneurial goals.

b) Identify resources (books, courses, mentors) that can help you develop these skills.

c) Create a learning schedule for the next three months, dedicating specific time each week to skill development.

12. Accountability System:

Ensuring follow-through on your commitments:

a) Choose an accountability partner - someone who can support you and hold you responsible for your goals.

b) Set up a regular check-in schedule with your accountability partner.

c) Determine how you will track and measure your progress on your various goals and initiatives.

13. Resilience Strategy:

Preparing for challenges and setbacks:

a) Reflect on past setbacks and identify three key lessons or strategies that helped you overcome them.

b) Create a personal mantra or affirmation that you can use to stay motivated during difficult times.

c) Develop a self-care plan to ensure you're taking care of your physical and mental health as you pursue your goals.

14. Financial Planning:

Ensuring the sustainability of your entrepreneurial journey:

a) Review your current financial situation and create a budget that aligns with your business goals.

b) Identify potential sources of funding or investment for your business initiatives.

c) Develop a financial contingency plan for potential setbacks or unexpected expenses.

15. Impact Measurement:

Assessing the difference you're making:

a) Define what success looks like for you beyond financial metrics.

b) Establish three key performance indicators (KPIs) that will help you measure your impact on your clients, community, or industry.

c) Create a system for regularly reviewing and reflecting on these impact metrics.

16. Time Management:

Applying the "Every Second Counts" principle:

a) Track your time for a week to identify where you're spending most of your energy.

b) Identify three time-wasting activities you can eliminate or reduce.

c) Create a ideal weekly schedule that prioritizes your most important tasks and goals.

17. Personal Brand Development:

Packaging yourself and your business effectively:

a) Define the core values and qualities you want your personal brand to convey.

b) Audit your online presence (social media, website, etc.) and identify three ways you can better align it with your desired brand image.

c) Develop a content creation plan to regularly share your insights and story with your audience.

18. Partnership and Collaboration:

Leveraging the power of "We Are The 'They'":

a) Identify three potential partners or collaborators who share your values and could help you achieve your goals.

b) Develop a pitch or proposal for a collaborative project with one of these potential partners.

c) Plan a community event or initiative that brings together various stakeholders in your industry or community.

19. Innovation Pipeline:

Staying ahead of the curve:

a) Set up a system for staying informed about trends and developments in your industry.

b) Schedule regular brainstorming sessions to generate new ideas for your business.

c) Develop a process for evaluating and implementing new ideas.

20. Legacy Planning:

Thinking beyond immediate success:

a) Reflect on the long-term impact you want to have through your entrepreneurial journey.

b) Identify three ways you can start building that legacy now.

c) Create a mentorship or training program to pass on your knowledge and experiences to others.

21. Action Plan Integration:

Bringing it all together:

a) Review all the actions and initiatives you've identified in this exercise.

b) Prioritize these actions based on their potential impact and your current resources.

c) Create a 90-day action plan, detailing specific steps you'll take each week to move forward on your highest priority items.

CONCLUSION

Remember, this action plan is a living document. Review it regularly, celebrate your progress, learn from your setbacks, and adjust your plan as needed. The entrepreneurial journey is not a straight line, but with consistent effort and a commitment to learning and growth, you can make steady progress towards your goals.

As you implement this plan, keep in mind the overarching lesson of this book: your journey is unique, and your story has power. As you take these actions, think about how you can package and share your experiences in a way that inspires and uplifts others.

Your entrepreneurial journey is not just about building a successful business. It's about making a positive impact, about using your unique talents and experiences to create value for others. It's about writing a story with your life that inspires others to dream bigger and reach higher.

So go forth with courage and determination. Embrace the challenges as opportunities for growth. Celebrate your successes, learn from your failures, and always keep pushing forward. Remember, every step you take is not just advancing your own journey - it's blazing a trail for others to follow.

The world is waiting for the unique contribution that only you can make. With passion, purpose, and perseverance, you have the power to turn your entrepreneurial dreams into reality, to transform not just your own life, but the lives of those around you.

Your journey starts now. Embrace it, live it, share it. The future is bright, and you have the power to make it even brighter. Now go out there and make it happen!

ACKNOWLEDGEMENT

"Gratitude is not just about saying 'thank you' – it's about recognizing the inches of opportunity all around us, responding with urgency to show appreciation, and always raising our awareness of the positive impact others have on our journey. Every 'thank you' is a building block towards a better way, a reminder that we are all 'they' in this shared adventure of growth and success."

As I reflect on the journey that has led to this book, I am filled with immense gratitude for the countless individuals who have shaped my path and supported my vision. My story, from the streets of Detroit to the pages of this book, is not just my own – it is a testament to the power of community, mentorship, and unwavering belief in the potential for change.

First and foremost, I want to thank my family and the community that raised me. Growing up in Detroit, I witnessed firsthand the challenges that plagued our neighborhoods. But I also saw the resilience, creativity, and untapped potential that coursed through our streets. To my mother, who taught me the value of hard work and perseverance, and to the neighbors who looked out for me when times were tough – your love and support laid the foundation for everything I've achieved.

To the young men and women I grew up with, who faced the same difficult choices I did – this book is for you. I know the allure of quick money and the desperation that can drive us to make choices we later regret. But I hope my story serves as proof that there are other paths, other ways to make our mark on the world. You are more than your circumstances, more than the labels society may try to put on you. You have the power to rewrite your story, just as I have rewritten mine.

I must express my deepest appreciation to Dan Gilbert, a visionary entrepreneur whose impact on Detroit and the business world at large cannot be overstated. Dan, your commitment to revitalizing our city has been nothing short of transformative. You showed us that it's possible to build a thriving business while also uplifting the community around us. Your investments in Detroit's downtown have rippled out to the neighborhoods, creating opportunities and breathing new life into our city.

Dan, your approach to business and community development has been a beacon of inspiration for entrepreneurs like myself. You've shown us that success isn't just about personal gain, but about creating value for others and leaving a lasting positive impact on our communities. Your vision of building Detroit "from the inside out" resonates deeply with my own mission to revitalize our neighborhoods and create opportunities for those who have been overlooked.

I am particularly grateful for the ISMs that have become a cornerstone of the culture at Rocket Companies®. These guiding principles, which I've had the honor of incorporating into this book, have provided a roadmap not just for business success, but for personal growth and community impact. They remind us to always raise our level of awareness, to find the inches we need everywhere around us, and to respond with a sense of urgency. These ISMs have become more than just corporate values – they are a philosophy for life and leadership that can transform individuals and communities.

To the team at Rocket Companies®, thank you for embodying these ISMs and showing the world what's possible when a company truly commits to excellence and community impact. Your culture of innovation, service, and community engagement sets a new standard for what business can and should be in the 21st century.

Dan, your emphasis on retaining young talent in Detroit by focusing on their needs – from regional transportation to entertainment and affordable housing – aligns perfectly with my own mission to create opportunities for the next generation. You've shown us that revitalizing a city isn't just about buildings and businesses, but about creating an ecosystem where talent can thrive.

To all the entrepreneurs out there, especially those from challenging backgrounds who might doubt their place in the business world – let Dan Gilbert's story, and indeed my own, be a reminder that your past does not determine your future. With vision, determination, and a commitment to serving others, you can not only build successful businesses but also be catalysts for positive change in your communities.

Finally, to my team at Believe Cleaning, our clients, and everyone who has been part of this incredible journey – thank you. Your trust, hard work, and belief in our mission have made all of this possible. We're not just cleaning buildings; we're cleaning up the business world and revitalizing communities, one opportunity at a time.

As we close this book, let us remember that our work is far from over. The story of Detroit's renaissance, like the story of any individual or community rising from adversity, is still being written. And each of us, with our unique talents and perspectives, has a role to play in shaping that story.

To Dan Gilbert, to Detroit, and to dreamers everywhere – this book is for you. Let's continue to believe, to build, and to make a difference, one day at a time.

With deepest gratitude,

Mario Kelly

Mario Kelly

Made in the USA
Middletown, DE
12 April 2025